ABOUT THE A

Pia Pasternack

After 20 years of marriage and three children, full-time mum Pia Pasternack came home one day to find a note on the doormat and her husband gone. Heartbroken, this was the first of a series of revelations that left her and her family reeling. Gradually, she built herself back up, and in *Making Peace with Divorce*, her first book, Pia passes on the lessons she, her friend Sarah Rayner and others have learned about the legal, financial and emotional implications of separation.

Pia and Sarah were school friends back in the days of the Boomtown Rats, and were delighted to reconnect recently and find they still get on like a house on fire. You can get in touch with Pia via **facebook/groups/makingfriendswithdivorce**.

Sarah Rayner

Sarah Rayner is the author of five novels including the international bestseller, *One Moment, One Morning* and the two follow-ups, *The Two Week Wait* and *Another Night, Another Day*. In 2014 she published *Making Friends with Anxiety, a warm, supportive little book to help ease worry and panic.* This was followed by a series of books including *Making Friends with the Menopause* and *Making Friends with Depression*. In 2017 Sarah set up the small press, **creativepumpkinpublishing.com** and invited Pia to write for the new imprint. *Making Friends with Divorce* is the result of that suggestion.

After a brief marriage, Sarah separated from her first husband in 2005. She met Tom, to whom she is now married, in 2007 and they live in Brighton. You can get in touch with Sarah via Facebook, Twitter and Instagram, all accessible through her website, **sarah-rayner.com**.

NON-FICTION BY SARAH RAYNER
Making Friends: A series of warm, supportive guides to help you on life's journey

BY SARAH RAYNER
Making Friends with Anxiety:
A warm, supportive little book to help ease worry and panic

More Making Friends with Anxiety:
A little book of creative activities to help reduce stress and worries

BY SARAH RAYNER AND DR PATRICK FITZGERALD
Making Friends with the Menopause:
A clear and comforting guide to support you as your body changes

Making Peace with the End of Life:
A clear and comforting guide to help you live well to the last

BY SARAH RAYNER, KATE HARRISON AND DR PATRICK FITZGERALD
Making Friends with Depression:
A warm and wise companion to recovery

BY SARAH RAYNER AND TRACEY SAINSBURY
Making Friends with your Fertility:
A clear and comforting guide to reproductive health

BY SARAH RAYNER AND JULES MILLER
Making Friends with Anxiety:
A Calming Colouring Book

NOVELS BY SARAH RAYNER

Another Night, Another Day
The Two Week Wait
One Moment, One Morning
Getting Even
The Other Half

This edition first published in 2017 by Creative Pumpkin Publishing, an imprint of The Creative Pumpkin Ltd., 5 Howard Terrace, Brighton, East Sussex, BN1 3TR.
www.creativepumpkinpublishing.com

Creative Pumpkin
Publishing

First Edition October 2017

ISBN: 9780995794870

Cover design and illustrations: © Sarah Rayner.

Publisher's Note:
While the advice and information in the book are believed to be accurate and true at the time of going to press, neither of the authors can accept any legal responsibility or liability for any errors or omissions that may have been made.

PIA PASTERNACK
SARAH RAYNER

Making Peace
with Divorce

A warm, supportive guide to separating and starting anew,
offering guidance on legal, financial and family issues, helping
you through the emotional upheaval and out the other side

Featuring illustrations by Sarah Rayner

HELLO AND WELCOME

Imagine you are sitting at a table in your favourite restaurant and the waiter puts a whole watermelon in front of you with a flourish. You didn't order it, you don't want it, you don't like watermelon at all, and yet somehow, in this nightmare, you are going to have to eat it up. You can't consume it whole, though some people are staring at you as though they think you should. All you can do is slice it and tackle it in bite-sized pieces. Divorce is like that watermelon, unfortunately. It's big. And you have to swallow it. But we hope that we can help you to avoid most of the pips.

It's as well to size up the whole of it for a moment before you begin. Yes, separating *is* a big deal. It will have huge implications for many aspects of your life, and you may have worries about everything from who will take the spiders out of the bath or knowing how to make dinner if your partner always did, to where you are going to live or how you will be able to pay the bills when one household becomes two.

1

You may think you can't live without your partner or wonder whether you can live alone. Perhaps you fear you will never trust or be intimate with anyone ever again, or be hugged or have sex. At the same time your mind may be filled with unwelcome images of your partner enjoying all the intimacies you two once did – with someone else.

And it doesn't end there, not by any stretch, whether you or your partner is the one who has initiated the break up.

As well as losing your other half, you may very well lose your in-laws, some friends and possibly your home. Even (especially if you worked together) your job. You'll almost certainly fear for your children, if you have any, feeling that they will lose the security of the family life they have enjoyed until now.

You may be feeling completely overwhelmed by the vast unknown of what lies ahead, and terrified to make a move. You may fear that you are going mad.

'I remember well the "washing machine mind" that had things spinning round and round, day and night, and feeling I had nothing to grasp hold of.' **Lucy**

People will be giving you conflicting advice about what you should do, what your ex is going to do, and whether any of it is reasonable. In the meantime, if you have children, they may of course be utterly distraught themselves. So while you want to curl up and die, you need more than ever to be strong and supportive for them. If only you knew how to comfort them when, in fact, the future is a vast unknown and possibly one in which one parent or both has hurt them very much.

And now, into this maelstrom, there are all these forms to fill. So many critical details to think about, just when you may be totally heartbroken and barely able to function, or living on a friend's sofa with only an ancient mobile on which to research how to unravel the mess! No wonder it can seem overwhelming. But you *can* disentangle yourself. Thousands – millions! – of couples have, and not all of them are bitter, miserable or consider they've lost more than they've gained once the dust has settled. It's possible to come out with your head held high. So, let's take a deep breath and break it down.

In the following chapters we tackle:

- **Decision** – to stay or go, to petition or not
- **Impact** – what effects you can expect, and help dealing with them
- **Vacating the Relationship** – what needs to be done to disentangle your lives
- **Other People** – how to talk to your ex, your children and others about the split
- **Representation** – ratifying a divorce: which route to go down and how to choose a lawyer
- **Conflict** – what if things don't go smoothly?
- **Emergence** – how to make a great future for yourself after separation

I'd be the first to tell you that it takes (at least) two people to make a good divorce and I would be lying if I said that mine was good. What I can say is that I learned an awful lot. I have learned more about myself in the few years since my separation than in all the many before. And, like many others I have encountered, I have gone from feeling suicidal at the loss of my soul mate and marriage, to feeling grateful that it happened.

We had just celebrated our 20th wedding anniversary with a weekend away. Back in France, where we'd first met, and away from the distractions of the daily grind, we enjoyed one another's company. Almost a second honeymoon. After a rocky few years, things were looking up. So I had a spring in my step when I came home from my course one day. It was the day of our first counselling session and I was excited at the promise of further improvements in our relationship. I put down my shopping to pick up the post and that's when I saw the envelope with my name in his handwriting. He'd gone. My devastation was complete, but there was worse to come. It turned out there had been secrets for some time, mostly of a financial nature. These emerged gradually over a couple of years during which the man I married also revealed himself to be very different from what I'd thought. I had no income at all, and was left with an enormous mortgage and three children in private schools. It was a lot to deal with for someone who didn't think she could live without him, and didn't want to. I fell apart physically and mentally. Our divorce was not straightforward and I did not cope with it well.

Despite the pain and hardship all round, however, and much that I regret, our split has turned out to be for the best. In the early days, I heard others say much the same, and I never thought it would be true for me. I hope that, together with Sarah, who has edited and illustrated this book, I can help you to get to the same point.

There are many books on divorce, so why bother with this one?

1. I've been there.

2. Sarah has been there, too. Not only has she been through a divorce that was very different from mine, but her mum and dad split up as well. 'I was often caught in the middle of two warring parents,' she says, and we hope her perspective on what it can feel like for a child is useful.

3. It's short, and to the point – deliberately so. We haven't tried to answer every question you might have, or counsel you on the specifics of your situation. A lot of information can be overwhelming, and we don't want to add to your confusion at a time when (if you're anything like me) you are finding it difficult to concentrate. As with all the books in the *Making Friends*[1] series, *Making Peace with Divorce* aims to give you a clear overview of the main issues. We'll explore the legal, financial and familial implications – with pointers on where to get more information should you need it. We'll also look at the emotional fall out, and make some suggestions that we hope will add grist to your mill as you move forward into the future.

4. This book aims to feel like a chat with a friend… Sarah and I met in school – back when we were seven years old. Even then, we could talk for England! So whilst we've tried to be concise and clear, we've also tried to be supportive.

I was once advised by a wise man that one day I would 'walk out into the sunshine'. One day you will join me there.

CONTENTS

3. 'V' is for Vacating the Relationship
What needs to be done to disentangle your lives
- Getting help
  - Friends and family
  - Professional help
  - Free help and support online
- The marital pot
  - Your home
  - Income
  - Financial disassociation
- Other legalities
  - Your name
  - Your will
  - Lasting power of attorney
  - Next of kin
  - Notifying authorities
- Children
  - Managing the separation well for your children
  - Housing children
  - A Parenting Plan
  - Money for children

4. 'O' is for Other People
How to talk to your ex, your children and others about the split
- Communicating with your ex
  - 'No Contact Rule'
  - Language
  - Responding
  - Social media
  - Meeting
- Communicating with the children
  - Breaking the news
  - During the divorce and after
  - Counselling for kids
  - Introducing new partners
- Communicating with others
- Communicating with yourself

5. 'R' is for Representation

Ratifying a divorce: which route to go down and how to choose a lawyer

- Petitioning for divorce
  - If you want to begin the divorce
  - Unreasonable Behaviour
  - Submitting the form
  - If you are the Respondent
- Completing Form E
  - Section 1 – General Information
  - Section 2 – Financial Details
  - Section 3 – Financial Requirements
  - Section 4 – Other Information
  - Section 5 – Order Sought
  - A word about spousal maintenance
  - A word about child maintenance
  - Statement of Truth
- Do I need a lawyer?
  - Doing without a lawyer
    - > Representing yourself in court
  - Nearly doing without a lawyer
    - > Quickie online divorce
    - > Fixed price divorce
    - > Using a lawyer ad hoc
- How to choose a lawyer
  - Choosing a solicitor
  - Choosing a barrister
  - Types of lawyers and types of process
    - > Collaboration
    - > Mediation
- Paying for a lawyer
  - How lawyers charge
  - How much will it cost?
  - Affording legal help

6. 'C' is for Conflict
What if things don't go smoothly?

- Going to court
  - What to expect
- Fighting over money
  - First Directions Appointment
  - Financial Dispute Resolution Hearing
  - Final Hearing
  - Maintenance Pending Suit
- Fighting over children
  - Child Arrangement Orders
  - Specific Issue Orders
  - Prohibited Steps Order
  - Child Arrangements Programme
  - Child Contact Interventions
- Enforcing a Court Order
  - Enforcing child arrangements
  - Enforcing financial arrangements
- Next steps – all about the future

7. 'E' is for Emergence
How to make a great future for yourself after separation

- Stories from others who've been there
- Making a new life
- Reframing failure
- Working on pulling your 'self' together
  - Therapy
  - Pursuing interests old and new
  - Having a social life
  - To stay single or to try dating?
  - Meeting a significant other
  - Where to meet someone
  - Internet dating pointers
- Holidays
- Festivities
- Looking on the bright side

- Looking forward and back
- Conclusion – living happily

Join the conversation
Acknowledgements
Useful websites
Endnotes
Recommended reading
Other books by Sarah Rayner
- *Making Friends with Anxiety*
- *Making Friends with your Fertility*
- *Making Friends with the Menopause*
- *Making Friends with Depression*
- *Making Peace with the End of Life*
- *One Moment, One Morning*
- *The Two Week Wait*
- *Another Night, Another Day*

1. 'D' IS FOR DECISIONS
TO STAY OR GO, TO PETITION OR NOT

The decision to divorce is a HUGE one. Even if you never formalised your relationship with a ceremony, leaving a long-term partner is rarely easy and, since you are reading this book, I hope you'll forgive the assumption that you're here to get help, whether in making your decision and carrying it through, or in dealing with the decision made by your partner.

While divorce is more common than in our parents' day (42% of marriages in the UK[2], with similar figures elsewhere in the Western world) we all start out thinking it won't happen to us, and ending a long-term partnership can seem a big personal failure.

> *'My fiancé and I were together for a long time, but we never made it to the altar because just short of our wedding he told me he felt he had to return to his ex. My world ended that day and in many ways I still haven't recovered from it. There were so many losses that resulted from that decision: loss of a dream, loss of life partner, home, community, career – it just went on and on.'* **Helen**

Whether splitting up is something you are considering or your partner has sprung it on you, there is much to negotiate. We will be helping you to tackle the various aspects of untangling your relationship in forthcoming chapters. But first there is one burning question to answer, before you start unravelling anything at all.

1.1 Should you stay or go?

Let's kick off with the most fundamental decision: should you stay in the relationship, or leave? If you are the one thinking about ending the marriage, you may well be finding the situation hard. Perhaps you are having an affair and the prospect of leaving a dreary marriage for your new love is exciting, or maybe you are escaping an abusive relationship and know deep down that ending it is for the best. Whatever the circumstances, changing the status quo can be difficult, especially when children are involved.

> *'It took me four attempts before I finally left my husband after 18 years. I'd been desperate to get away but he was extremely controlling, and my simply "wanting to leave" wasn't considered a good enough reason to break up the family. I eventually found the courage when I discovered he had a secret "friendship" with another woman. At last I had a reason he couldn't argue with – he knew that he couldn't cajole me back from that one.'* **Maggie**

Even if you want to split up, the prospect of hurting your partner might feel so daunting that you can't make the first move.

> *'I'm unhappy and no longer in love with my wife. There isn't anyone else, I just don't want to be in this marriage any more. And yet I don't know how to tell her that. I don't think she will take it well, and I can't face the pain and arguments.'* **Marcus**

It's equally possible that your partner is having an affair and you are wondering whether to forgive and try again. Perhaps you feel you should stay together 'for the sake of the kids'.

'My marriage isn't great and I suspect he sleeps around. But whenever I think about our little boy, I feel I have to put up with it.' **Maria**

Ultimately, of course, only you can decide, but that doesn't mean you have to make the decision all on your own. To support you in your decision-making, there is help in the form of:

- Counselling
- Talking to friends and family
- Reading and researching the issues, options and implications
- Taking legal advice

In this chapter we're going to focus on the first in this list. We'll be turning to the subject of legal advice in later chapters. You can also find a list of recommended reading at the end, as you may find Googling specific questions brings up more information than you can handle. As for talking to friends, it's true that many people who know you well will be able to offer advice, and most of those who have been in similar situations can warn you about the pitfalls and reassure you. A word of caution however: 'Friends and family may bring their own baggage on marriage into advising you on yours,' says Sarah. 'I noticed this when my husband and I were separating, and some of those who I thought would have my back proved very judgemental. Bear in mind that objectivity is rare. If someone's own marriage is miserable yet they're committed to staying, that may well be reflected in what they suggest you should do.'

'A friend rang me from the US, and spent an hour – on an international call – insisting I must do everything I could to save my marriage (even though my husband was abusive). She was one of several people I allowed to persuade me, against my gut-instinct, to stay. A year later she left her own husband. Her reasons for leaving were completely justified too, but it took me a while to stop feeling bitter about the influence she'd had on me. It took me another four years to get out. Seek advice, for sure, but pay most attention to your gut instinct.' **Maggie**

There are people who should be more objective, however – counsellors and therapists. Which leads me neatly to…

1.2 Should you try couples' counselling?

I'll cut to the chase: in my opinion, counselling is *always* a good idea. I would urge you, since you are reading a book about divorce, to consider it, *even if both parties are in favour of separating.* Especially if you have children: the help you get in communicating with one another can make a huge difference to the happiness of all concerned.

Many people believe that 'marriage guidance counsellors' are there to keep couples together. Not true! Our counsellor explained this to me and my husband right at the outset (I remember being upset by it at the time). Please don't let this misconception deter you or your partner from agreeing to go.

Furthermore (and this is not a trivial point) using a counsellor as a means to communicate between the two of you is vastly cheaper than having the same discussions through two sets of lawyers, and far less confrontational.

1.2i Saving the marriage

If you think that there is any chance that the relationship can be saved, you both stand to gain from putting any doubts about counselling to one side. If your partner is afraid or unwilling to attend with you, perhaps you can explain that counselling will be helpful no matter what emerges, or what you both decide to do. You might want to say that you are keen to hear your partner's side of the story and to understand his or her point of view. And if that fails, consider going on your own.

It's true a counsellor *might* not be able to help – counsellors vary in skill, plus the fit between professional and clients is as individual as the participants – but marriages can be saved from the doldrums, whether caused by boredom or infidelity, if both parties are willing to do what it takes. Of course, not all marriages can be saved by seeing a counsellor – nor should they: in some cases the two of you will be incompatible or your differences too great. If this is the case, the counsellor will be able to help you manage the separation.

Counsellors are trained and experienced, and one of the key benefits of talking in their presence is that they can help to ensure that both of you feel able to express how you feel, and – equally importantly – that each of you hears what the other is saying. Even if your situation seems so complex there's no way you can unravel it, counselling can be invaluable, giving you insights you'd never reach alone and helping you come to a new understanding of one another. (You can read more about counselling and how it differs from psychotherapy[3].)

'When I was diagnosed with cancer, my husband behaved appallingly. He refused to talk about my diagnosis, didn't offer to drive me to hospital and at one point even asked for a divorce. I was devastated – I was going through enough as it was. But I was also mystified, as though we've had our ups and downs, his response was uncharacteristically harsh. So I insisted we went to counselling. Over the course of several sessions, we worked out that my husband was in denial about my illness. Instead of facing his fears and his upset so he could support me, his reactions had become skewed. He'd never have seen this without help – he simply wasn't listening to me at this time, and without a third party to mediate, I'm not sure we'd have found a way through.' **Sylvia**

1.2ii Should you take your partner back?

If your partner has strayed, or been violent, or broken another promise to stay sober, or in some other way had his or her last chance, but is begging for another, what to do? This is very much up to the individual, of course. Nonetheless, I offer a personal insight. For many years I have been an active member of Wikivorce[4], an excellent online source of information and support. Time and again members talked about 'the first time I took her back' or 'the second time he went'. There may have been stories I didn't hear, because it all ended happily. But I also noticed how many thought that they could patch things up and finally acknowledged they'd been wrong. (And that's when the partner was willing to return, which was not always the case.) All too often those who fought to give it another go with an erring partner ended up wishing that they had finished it sooner.

> *'I was stuck in fear of what my future would be. How would I cope? Financial uncertainty was a big thing for me. I had no vision of what my life would look like, and this kept me stuck for years in a toxic relationship. But finally, I got to the point when I'd had enough. Then I just cut and ran.'* **Sue**

If this sounds familiar, you probably know yourself already, deep down, that your partner is not going to change. Yet the alternative may be too awful to contemplate. You may prefer the devil you know than to break up the family unit for the great unknown with all the fallout and uncertainty and hurt that entails. Familiarity is comforting. And you want to believe that, this time, he or she means it.

> *'Don't cling to a mistake just because you spent a lot of time making it.'* **Phil**

Here, again, I'd recommend counselling to help you think things through, whether with your partner or alone. I used to believe that staying together, whether for the sake of the children, or because of a vow, or for any reason, was a good thing. I've changed my mind. I now feel that marriage contracts would be far better if there was open acknowledgment that the union may not be 'till death do us part' so that, if things unravel, it is not seen as such a failure[5]. If you were brought up in a very traditional or religious community, such failure may be even harder to contemplate. Yet help is available and you may find understanding counsellors can help you to know your own mind amongst all the confusion and expectations.

'Ostensibly, my wife and I split up because she had an affair. When she told me, I was devastated. She was clear that even though she still loved me, there was no way back. The irony was, a few months earlier, I'd seen a sign up in the local Citizens Advice Bureau for Relate, and thought: we should do that. *But I never pursued it. I was too ashamed and embarrassed. Now I wish I had done. She'd not met her new partner at that point and we might have found a way to sort our issues out.'* **Rich**

1.2iii Ending the marriage

If you feel sure there is no chance the marriage can be saved, counselling can still help. Please don't think that because you have made up your mind to divorce, there is no point in going. They are not there to force you to stay together, nor will you somehow be 'bullied' into giving it another go. Where appropriate, counsellors can play a very valuable part in helping you to separate as painlessly as possible.

Naturally, couples' counselling is only effective where both parties are willing to attend and to tell the truth, and I know that this cannot always be achieved. My husband left me on the day we were to have had our first session and refused to come. However he did come to meetings afterwards. My experience of counselling was that, although he continued to deceive me and the counsellor in important ways, certain issues did get aired nonetheless. Even when secrets and lies remained, it was still useful in the breakdown of the relationship, when communication was fraught or non-existent, to have a place to meet once a week for necessary discussions in the presence of a referee! We both were given opportunity to speak and helped to listen. There was an independent witness to the discussion, who might challenge or defend us, and who stopped things from escalating, or breaking down altogether.

1.2iv How to find a reputable counsellor

Relate
Probably the best-known brand, Relate is the UK's largest provider of relationship support, and (as it says on their website www.relate.org.uk) 'every year we help over a million people of all ages, backgrounds and sexual orientations to strengthen their relationships'. They have Relate Centres up and down the country, as well as licensed local counsellors, and can also offer help via phone, email and live chat.

Counselling Directory, BACP and the UKCP
Counselling-directory.org.uk allows you to search a database of professional therapists by location and type of counselling, including for couples. The two main professional bodies for psychotherapists and counsellors in the UK are The British Association of Counsellors and Psychotherapists (bacp.co.uk) and

the UK Council for Psychotherapy (psychotherapy.org.uk). Please check that anyone you consult has professional accreditation.

Google
Don't dismiss Google: a quick search for couples or relationship counselling throws up plenty of other therapy centres and individual counsellors near you; most of these will be qualified but you may want to check.

Your doctor
Though free help is not always available, it's worth trying your GP for a referral. We received a year's free couple's counselling on the NHS from the excellent Tavistock Centre in London, a short walk from our home.

Your friends
Not everybody feels comfortable discussing their intimate relationships or admitting to having had help, but if you open up to your friends, you may well find that others have been in a similar boat and can refer sources of help or individual counsellors. Personal recommendations are always valuable, though a counsellor who suits your friend might not suit you. Don't forget that the counsellors will keep any information about you and your friend completely confidential.

1.3 Accepting the decision

Marriages can – especially with the help of counselling – survive rocky periods and infidelity, if both partners are willing. The sad fact, though, is that if one of you has definitely decided it's over, it is. I know from bitter experience that this can be hard to accept. Like many who have been left seemingly out of the blue, I persisted for some time in thinking that my ex was making a mistake and would surely come to his senses one day soon. It's easy to believe that if we are understanding, or forgive or change (nag less, tidy up more, lose weight, whatever) we can fix it. In this way, many have been known to give adulterers / alcoholics / abusers / absconders a second or third chance. Sadly, though you may feel yours would be the exception that proves the rule, these marriages usually fail, but over a longer period and with greater pain and recrimination. There is a difference between a rocky patch and someone deciding it's over. I'll say it again: if one of you has decided it's over, it is[6]. You cannot force your partner to love you, to come back, or stay, no matter what you do, and futile attempts to do so will merely prolong the agony.

You may not want to accept this. I did not. In my own case, there was a great big 'D' for Disbelief. For a very long time I was convinced that my husband was having a midlife crisis, that I could help him out of it, that he would soon come to his senses and realise that the whole thing was a hideous mistake, and even that this would bring us closer together.

FACT: If your partner wants a separation, then BY DEFINITION your relationship is not a good one. The sooner you can come to terms with this the better.

If I knew how to accelerate this acceptance, I would tell you. I don't. What I can say is that most people, in my experience, achieve acceptance in the end, and when they do, the sadness and anger subsides and they make peace with the new reality, seeing the end of the relationship as inevitable or even as a good thing.

'I found it helpful to have sessions with a psychologist to talk about the separation and also reflect on why we stayed in this relationship as long as we did. It was uncomfortable but worth it.' **Andy**

'Over time, with help from a counsellor, I began to realise that our relationship and its painful end were simply the result of our limitations, both his and mine. I have grown stronger and happier in ways I never would have if we had stayed together.' **Suzie**

Whether or not the two of you have relationship counselling, it may very well be worth your seeing someone on your own to help you come to terms with the new reality. Maybe you didn't want it, but you are stuck with it. I didn't want it either – I fought to save my marriage, as many do. It was a losing battle, as it often is, but ultimately, it wasn't an unhappy ending.

TIP: If your partner assures you that there is no one else, be prepared for a surprise.

If I had a pound for every time someone joined Wikivorce saying that there was nobody else involved, only for it to turn out later that their partner had been having an affair and that the new love was waiting in the wings… well, it would have made quite a dent in the cost of my divorce!

1.4 So, let's go back to the original decision: is it time to call it a day?

If you've been thinking about divorce and definitely want to proceed, and your partner is in the dark, I would urge you to be honest, fair, kind, and generous. This will reap rewards in the end for your relationship with your ex, any children, and any other friends and relations who get drawn in. Importantly, it will help you to feel better about yourself. If this is going to come as a bombshell, give your partner time to adjust. Suggest and agree to counselling to make the whole process as painless as possible.

If, on the other hand, the spectre of divorce has been visited upon you against your will, you still have plenty of decisions to make about how you are going to react. One of them is whether to petition for a divorce you never wanted. In the end, I did this, rather than wait for the axe to fall. I still thought I would wake up to find it had all been a bad dream but I set the wheels in motion anyway, which, as it turns out, was a good thing.

Sometimes both partners agree that their relationship has run its course. Divorces can then be perfectly civilized, amicable and cheap. But this is very rare. So for the rest of this book, we will assume that at least one of you has decided to end the relationship and at least one of you has decided to make it official. And that, if neither of those is you, you are nonetheless going to try to accept the situation and prepare yourself as best you can for the road ahead.

2. 'I' IS FOR IMPACT
WHAT EFFECTS YOU CAN EXPECT, AND HELP DEALING WITH THEM

When my husband left, I was literally *blindsided*. Stumbling around in the dark. Over a period of a few months my sight got worse and worse until I had to have surgery to replace my lenses with artificial ones. I also lost my hair, and my concentration. Anxiety, depression, agoraphobia, memory loss, insomnia, clumsiness, even incontinence…

Quite often (as in my case) divorce hits at the same time as the menopause, with its various physical and emotional upheavals. Just when you think things can't possibly get any worse, when you are struggling to decide what to say to your lawyers, to read what they send you, to bend your mind round the finances, or to find somewhere to live, possibly while also trying to support your children, and maybe elderly parents as well, not to mention an actual job, you may find you can't cope mentally or physically. It can be that stressful. Many of us (especially those who have maybe relied too much on our partners and not enough on ourselves?) feel as though we are falling apart. We can't think straight, we can't sleep, we can't eat. Sometimes it can seem as though we have reverted to toddlers who want our mummies – we feel that vulnerable and helpless. I did.

'When my husband told me he was leaving, the effect was absolutely cataclysmic. Everything changed, everything! And all for the worse. All I could think of was that I wished I was dead.' **Jane**

So I'm not going to beat about the bush: for lots of people, the impact of separation will be enormous and possibly all encompassing, especially if the relationship was a long one, if the partners had very defined roles, if you tended to do things together and/or if money is tight. If you've been forced into this situation against your will or out of the blue, there may be shock and disbelief to cope with as well. For many, these changes will, at least in the short term, be negative. But please **do not give up hope!** Some good will very likely come of this, even if right now you can't believe it.

2.1 Divorce and loss

It is often said that divorce is similar to bereavement, that one has to mourn the loss of the relationship, and that the grief one experiences goes through the same stages famously described in 1969 by Elisabeth Kübler-Ross[7]:

- Denial
- Anger
- Bargaining
- Depression
- Acceptance

Though these stages are not clear-cut, do not necessarily fall neatly into order, and often repeat, the list provides a useful guide as to what to expect. Forewarned is forearmed. If you know what might hit you, you're less likely to think that you are going mad or that these overwhelming feelings will last forever.

TIP: Don't be afraid to experience negative emotions. Recognise that most of them are fed by your understandable fear of the unknown and trust that they will pass.

If you've been in an unhappy relationship, your initial feeling may be one of euphoria at having escaped. You might find that you fluctuate wildly at first between glee and remorse.

'Because I instigated the separation, I thought these emotions wouldn't hit me. But they did. I stopped eating. I dropped to a size 8 – not a good size for me – and started drinking a lot of alcohol. I went hyper. I was out partying all the time. It was if I'd been held back for so long that, like a slingshot pulled taught, when I was released – WHOOSH! – I went supersonic.' **Sue**

If you're keen to find a safe space to vent your spleen, express your sorrow or any other emotions you may be feeling, **you might like to join our group on Facebook**[8]. You have to ask to join because *Making Peace with Divorce* is a 'closed' group to keep the posts confidential. (This means your posts are only visible to other members of the group and not to your other Facebook friends or family members.)

TIP: Ask for help when you can't cope.

'I don't know where to start. My whole world has turned upside down and my head is whirling, never mind my heart, which is in pieces.' **Edward**

Asking for help does not come easily to many of us. Friends and family will want to support you, but may be unsure of what you need, and afraid to intrude on your grief. Sometimes just having someone with you in a stressful situation – such as when you go to collect your things, or open a letter from your lawyer – can make a it more manageable.

And on those days when you are *really* struggling and don't feel strong enough to talk to anyone – even online – **remember to be kind to yourself, first and foremost.**

2.2 Denial

Often the early days of separation are characterised by denial or disbelief. And it is hardly surprising if everything feels unreal when the behaviour of your ex is uncharacteristic and unexpected.

'We were sitting down to dinner and my wife told me she didn't love me. That was six months ago and I still can't quite believe it.' **Sam**

'He was always such a loving husband, I don't know who this new person is.' **Julie**

'My ex turned into an alien overnight!' **Alex**

I know I'm not alone in believing for a long time that my ex was having some kind of mid-life crisis and that he would surely come to his senses any day. Many spouses report the same. One of the children persisted in the belief (backed up by online research) that their father had a brain tumour or had received a blow to the head. When the event is very shocking, it is natural to find it difficult to believe, and therefore to deny what is happening. It upsets your world order and does not compute. You can't believe it because it goes against everything you know.

'My supersonic self was my real self, but I had been pretending for so long that with hindsight I can see that to my husband, whom I had left, it must have seemed as if I had morphed into another person.' **Sue**

In some cases, this stage will be prolonged by dithering on the part of the leaver, or false hope-giving.

TIP: Remember, if your partner has sprung this on you, he or she may have been planning for a while and will have had plenty of time to get used to the idea.

> *'He disappeared. I'd got £900 in the bank and four kids, and he disappeared. And that was it, really.'* **Carol**

One reason that you might struggle so much to believe what is happening, and to accept how your ex has changed, when suddenly faced with a request for divorce, the departure of your partner, or news of an affair: your ex has the advantage of time. You are playing catch up. You are reeling, confused, and upset. Your partner may seem steely: indeed he or she may have been steeling him or herself for a long time before feeling able to make this move.

TIP: If your partner is willing to explain, and you are willing to listen (again, a counsellor or mediator could be invaluable here), you may get some clarity.

> *'I held back from telling my husband I was unhappy for fear of hurting him. Which is ironic, as in the end it was much more painful, not less. Now I see it's important to keep conversations going in relationships, but back then I just fled.'* **Sue**

So clearly then, denial does not only affect the dumped but can also come into play with the one doing the dumping. Even if you left an abusive relationship, while the overwhelming feeling may be one of relief, there is also commonly a little voice questioning whether you needed to do this, whether you should have tried harder, or given one more chance.

> *'My husband was an alcoholic and I got caught up thinking "only I can fix him". Looking back, my married life was dreadful, with frequent drunken outbursts, some resulting in calls from me to the police. But part of me liked being the capable one, the saviour, and I did wonder whether I should have stayed to help him.'* **Juliet**

If you have a new love interest, it can be easy to deny the justifiable hurt and anger of the ex, children and wider family. 'What's the big deal?' you may be thinking, as you look at the world from your own cloud nine perspective. You may even be surprised that your ex is not happy for you.

TIP: If this sounds like you, a little empathy goes a long way.

Empathy for your ex means you don't deny the pain that you've caused him or her. It doesn't mean you have to return to the relationship or hand over all your worldly goods in a settlement. Nonetheless, empathy is a way of taking emotional responsibility.

2.2i Avoiding avoidance

Perhaps the most important thing to acknowledge here is that denial – sometimes called *avoidance*, is a coping mechanism. As such, it gives you time to adjust to – and thereby cope with – a distressing situation. Coping strategies can take all shapes and forms, and in the early stages of a split needn't be a cause for concern. To pour yourself a large whisky the night your spouse announces he or she is leaving, for instance, is very understandable. Equally, it seems fair enough to decide *not* to open a letter from a solicitor because you're on your way out to work and would rather wait until you've the headspace to cope with the contents. Coping strategies only become an issue when they're adopted with increasing frequency and depth and (ironically) prevent you from coping.

TIP: Try to recognise when you're drinking to avoid being in touch with feelings. Alcohol should be a treat, not a treatment.

Staying in denial can interfere with your ability to tackle challenges. It isn't always easy to tell if denial is holding you back, but it's important to realize your avoidance tactics won't change the reality of the situation. Drinking, drugs, sex, rebound relationships, throwing yourself into your work, or staying in bed: these are ways of avoiding facing the new reality and coming to terms with your feelings about it. Ultimately these submerged feelings will emerge in other ways, maybe in your next relationship, so try to face them, possibly with help from a counsellor.

For months I would say to my friends 'I can't believe he is doing this!' They would answer 'Well, he is' but it didn't sink in. (I confess I still sometimes find myself thinking this all these years later.) So I ignored advice to do anything to protect myself financially, which I now see was an expensive mistake.

'Your problem, Pia, is you keep thinking he is going to do the right thing. Well, he isn't.' **Helena**

TIP: Writing down thoughts can help with objectivity, so if, after a while, you're still struggling with facing reality, you might find keeping a journal helpful. (On the other hand, research[9] suggests that if you are the sort to mull things over too much, a journal can keep you stuck.)

Joining groups like the Making Peace with Divorce Facebook group allows you to post your feelings and get sensitive feedback from people who understand what you are going through. In addition, reading other people's stories can shine a surprisingly illuminating light on your own situation. There are support groups as well, for various different circumstances related to separation, for example Al Anon[10] for those who have been in a relationship with an alcoholic.

'Thanks for your support, everyone. It's good to come here and vent: my friends and family are fed up and keep telling me to move on.' **Peter**

TIP: We all get over things at different rates. It will take you as long as it takes.

2.3 Anger

Very often there are stages of being absolutely furious with your ex, even if he or she is *not* behaving appallingly (and many do).

If you instigated the separation because of a new relationship, you may feel frustrated that he or she is not 'getting with the programme', and seems to be holding things up or making unreasonable demands in terms of money or childcare or getting on with selling the house, which is now no longer your home but an asset to be realised.

If you left a violent relationship and are now in hiding or in a refuge, relieved to be away but missing your home comforts, friends, and family, you're likely to feel that your ex has forced this on you; anger and resentment are understandable.

As the one left behind, you may feel that life is likely to be more difficult, lonely, and poor, and blame your ex for that. Also for the damage you may feel is being done to your children; and for the fact that you have to deal with the fall out (paying for lawyers or facing moving house and so on) while your ex is continuing to enjoy the views from cloud nine.

2.3i Anger and negotiation

Many times I have seen or heard people voice absolutely murderous thoughts about their exes. It can get very vindictive and petty, even if you are normally relatively kind and placid. So what should you do with your anger instead? I've seen suggestions that it can be put to good use when standing up for yourself in negotiations or in court. I'm not convinced this is very helpful.

'When my ex demanded a large sum of money from me, I was furious. He knew I would struggle to find the cash and I felt he was making me pay for hurting him. But my mother gave wise counsel. She told me to bite my tongue and keep my fury from him. She has been through a divorce herself and learned the hard way that words expressed in anger rarely serve us.' **Sarah**

Going to court to negotiate when in a state of rage may make you more likely to entrench and refuse to compromise. And whilst you may not wish to find a middle ground, you will likely have to in order to reach an agreement.

TIP: Try – if you possibly can – to put your anger to one side when negotiating crucial issues such as childcare and maintenance and use a professional mediator if need be. You'll find guidance on how to find a mediator in Chapter 5.

2.3ii Managing your anger

If you're aware you've a short fuse when it comes to your ex, try to avoid conversational tactics that are likely to trigger anger in return, however tempting it might be.

Using phrases such as *always* (eg 'you always do that') and *never* ('you never listen to me') is a bad idea. It infers you're extrapolating a universal truth or permanent character flaw from a one-off incident.

31

Should or *shouldn't* can come across as dictatorial. ('You should see more of the kids', or 'You shouldn't be dating yet', for instance.) *Must* and *mustn't* and *ought* and *oughtn't* are similar.

TIP: There is more about how to talk to your ex (as well as children and others) in Chapter 4.

Acting out of anger is unlikely to help the situation; in extreme situations it could result in your partner or neighbours calling the police. It upsets everyone, sets a bad example for your children and will likely make you feel worse yourself when you calm down and regret your actions.

'Angry that she asked for a divorce, he burned their house down, police say. On Thursday, prosecutors [...] charged Joe Butler with first-degree arson. He pleaded not guilty and was jailed in lieu of $500,000. A court order bars him from coming within 1,000 feet of his wife.' **The News Tribune 17 August 2017**

TIP: If you're finding it difficult to have any sympathy with your ex, try thinking: *how would I feel if someone spoke like that to me?*

This said, rage is one of the hardest emotions to control. If you're having difficulties, there are further useful tips[11] on controlling anger on www.nhs.co.uk.

Finally, I might add that not everyone feels angry. I was often encouraged to feel angry but I didn't: just incredulous and despondent. For years after separation I felt overwhelming sadness, though I experienced a gamut of other emotions also.

2.4 Bargaining

Many wonder whether, if they change in some way, they can make everything all right again. When people told me to tell my ex where to stick it, or to move money so he couldn't, or to issue ultimatums, I said to them ever so sweetly, 'But no! Then he will never want to come back!' I may have been naïve, but I believed I was fighting for my children and marriage.

Maybe in a conscious or unconscious preference for the devil you know, you may believe tolerating deception, infidelity, indifference or violence is a price worth paying to keep the family together. So you make all kinds of offers, whether to your ex or to your god, in the hopes that you can preserve at least an outward appearance of a happy marriage. Or, as in my case, to avoid managing without your partner if the thought terrifies you and seems impossible.

'I honestly thought I could not live without him. I know it sounds silly, but it's true.' **Eliza**

Bargaining is an attempt to postpone, or even to turn back time; 'If I do XYZ, then my ex will love me again'. You might find yourself intensely focused on what you can do to change things, or what you or others could have done differently to prevent this situation. You may think about all the things that could have been and how wonderful life would have been, if only... I did this A LOT, and became quite fixated, for example, on the idea that my ex and I would never dandle grandchildren on our knees together.

'There is nothing either good or bad, but thinking makes it so.' **Hamlet**

It is an effort to hold onto what is lost, and, like denial and anger, a way to ease pain and avoid plunging into the unknown. Which leads us rather neatly into our next topic: *anxiety*.

2.5   Anxiety

Whilst the Kübler-Ross model is undoubtedly useful, it has limitations. No one experiences grief in neat stages – instead it tends to flow and come in waves – and not everyone gets through each stage never to experience it again. She herself wrote that she regretted writing about them in the way she did[12]. Plenty of people remain angry with their exes for the rest of their lives, and plenty of people experience anxiety – which isn't one of the classic stages she listed – when going through a relationship break-up.

> 'When my parents told me that they weren't getting on, I was about 12 years old. I remember my reaction was panic: I begged my father, "Please don't divorce!" I was very anxious about us losing our home. It took them a further six years to separate and, looking back, as a family that meant we were in limbo. But what I was really experiencing was fear of the unknown. This anxiety lingered and became a feature of my adulthood, but with psychotherapy and Mindfulness Based Cognitive Therapy I have learned to understand where much of it comes from and to manage it better.' **Sarah**

In her book *Making Friends with Anxiety*[13] Sarah explains in more detail how anxiety and panic are closely related to fear. The illustration below gives a summary.

What happens when we panic

HELP!

When we experience fear, we get a rush of adrenaline

Pupils dilate, mouth becomes dry, breathing gets faster and shallower.

Hard to see →

Difficult to swallow →

Heart pumps faster, neck and shoulders muscles tense

chest pains, shortness of breath, tingling

Liver releases stored sugar to provide fuel for energy

palpitations, high blood pressure

Bladder and anal muscles relax. Food and liquid are evacuated so we're lighter to run

indigestion, stomach cramps, nausea

frequent need to pee, diarrhoea

we sweat and blush.

Body cools itself by perspiring. Blood vessels move closer to the skin surface

Horribly scary symptoms ↑

The physical causes of those symptoms ↑

Our emotions don't exist only in the mind: they also reveal themselves physically, and the trauma of separation can force us into fight or flight mode with quite frightening and dramatic physical manifestations.

Note: One enormous piece of luck for me was that my ex left just after I started a three-year training course to be an Alexander Technique teacher. It is no exaggeration to say that this course saved my life. I like to think I would not have ended it all because of my children; all the same AT made an enormous difference to my ability to cope. Alexander Technique is a way of learning **embodied mindfulness**. It can help with aches and pains and posture, as is better known by the public. What is less well appreciated by people who have not tried it is that the means by which it achieves this involves a whole person approach, which has a beneficial effect on body and mind, so intimately entwined in ways we are just beginning to understand. If you are suffering from anxiety, headaches, insomnia or indeed if you just want to have greater ease in your life, I would urge you to try it. The website[14] of the Society of Teachers of the Alexander Technique (STAT) can help you find a teacher near you.

2.5i Panic attacks

These can be very common, especially in the early days. So many changes, so much fear of the unknown, not to mention possible court appearances and looming legal bills, and the distress of your children – it's hardly surprising that your anxiety can result in panic attacks. It's important to remember that even though it feels as though you are dying, nobody was ever killed by a panic attack. It will take a while but it will pass.

'I used to get panic attacks a lot, especially on my way to meet my ex. I remember finding it hard to breathe on the tube, with sweat pouring off me, and other passengers trying not to stare. So I arrived for meetings frightened, red faced and dishevelled, and felt completely disadvantaged.' **Polly**

TIP: By slowing the breathing and inhaling more deeply, we can bring down the heart rate and reduce the amount of adrenaline the body produces, which helps us to relax.

2.5ii Loss of appetite

Usually the only so-called benefit of this trauma is the 'divorce diet'. Many find they can't eat at all.

TIP: If you're finding it hard to stomach a full meal, try smoothies and yoghurts for relatively effortless calories. Ice cream is also good as because it is cold, it stimulates the taste buds. Remember the old adage 'little and often' and make sure you've a supply of tasty snacks to keep you going.

Also, don't be proud: accept help from friends if you can't face cooking. I will never forget the kindness of one who turned up unexpectedly on my doorstep with a prepared meal for the family, or of my mother who often did the same so we would have a home cooked dinner when I (previously a keen cook) struggled to keep things normal for the children and sometimes even found it hard to produce beans on toast.

(After this initial stage of rapid weight loss, like so many others I went to the opposite extreme with comfort eating, and gained back all the weight, and more.)

2.5iii Nausea

Related to loss of appetite, you may find you feel quite sick.

'For about six months, I vomited every single morning, first thing when I woke up. I suppose I just could not face the day.' **Angela**

Sometimes this very real nausea can be caused by unwelcome images of your ex in the arms of another and you may find yourself retching in Boots as you pass the contraceptives, but it can also be a response to general stress and anxiety. Your doctor may be able to give you something to help.

2.5iv Insomnia

This is a big issue for many. You may be unused to sleeping alone; the noises the house makes are suddenly terrifying and, anyway, there is so much spinning around in your mind, often the same question, over and over. I would fall asleep only to wake an hour or so later, drenched in sweat and with my mind racing. My GP gave me heavy-duty sleeping pills but they didn't stop me from waking in the night. Hot baths, relaxation tapes, white noise, meditation, lavender oil, milky drinks, and magnesium are all worth a try. But if you still have trouble, try not to worry too much. As I now know, it's astonishing how you can still function with very little sleep. And worrying about it only seems to make it worse.

FACT: While alcohol may help you to fall asleep, for a number of reasons (disturbed circadian rhythm, less REM sleep, more trips to the loo, snoring and sleep apnea) it will give you a more disturbed night.

2.6 Depression

This is a huge one. Whatever the reason for the divorce, you could find it triggers depression. Especially if you were not the one seeking to end the relationship, you are likely to feel that your world has been rocked, that you no longer know which way is up. You may even feel that your life is no longer worth living. (It is, and this feeling will pass, honestly.)

I suspect that many of us who have been unwillingly through the end of a serious relationship have suffered depression to a greater or lesser degree. Most of the separated people I know have been to their GP about this and taken prescription medicine and/or had therapy or counselling (or both) even if only briefly. It could be anything from weepiness and lethargy to full blown Post Traumatic Stress Disorder (which, while commonly associated with warfare, can also come into play in domestic life).

'My doctor explained that I was suffering from PTSD – I kept having flashbacks, could not sleep, was in a state of hyper-arousal waiting for the next bad thing, and suicidal.' **Pippa**

'The overwhelming sense of loss and pain is just relentless. I'm struggling terribly at the moment with everything.' **John**

It is entirely natural that you should feel sad at the end of a relationship but when it starts to affect your functioning and does not seem to be getting better, please remember that there is no shame in seeking medical help. Your doctor can prescribe medication to deal with depression and anxiety, and talking therapies including CBT (Cognitive Behaviour Therapy) to help you cope with your feelings.

There are other things you can do to help (exercise, keeping busy etc) but of course you are unlikely to feel up to doing them when you are depressed. For help with depression, you might like to read Sarah's book *Making Friends with Depression*. See p.185 for further sources of help.

TIP: You may find that your employer is supportive if you mention your home situation and any medication you are on.

2.7 Guilt and shame

While on our detour from Kübler-Ross's stages, let's examine guilt and shame, two further common responses to relationship breakdown.

'My ex was a heavy drinker, and I sensed his drinking was escalating, and began to fear he'd get violent with me as well as verbally abusive, so I finished the relationship. That was ten years ago and he has since died, of liver failure. Even though I'm married to someone else, I still feel guilty that I couldn't make it work, and wonder if, had I tried harder, he would still be here.' **Juliet**

'Although my wife was the one who effectively ended our marriage when she had an affair, I feel guilty that we couldn't make it work – not so much for me but for our children. She has asked me to leave but I feel our kids are better off living with us both, and it breaks my heart to split up the family.' **Hugh**

'Part of me thinks I deserve this, but the other part is so ashamed I'm in this situation.' **Nisha**

Some think of guilt as synonymous with shame, but clinical psychologist and psychoanalyst, Joseph Burgo, explains the difference succinctly[15]. He says that guilt is a feeling of responsibility or remorse for an offence or wrongdoing, and although the experience of guilt is painful, our ability to recognise that our own actions may have hurt someone, to empathise with that person's pain and to feel remorse for having caused it are all signs of emotional health.

> 'Not everyone who leaves a partner is callous about it. When my first marriage ended it was me who finished it. We'd not been married long and there were no children involved, but I felt very guilty at causing such pain. I genuinely like my ex-husband – he is a kind, good man, and I respect him too. Whilst I didn't want to be married to him any longer, I did feel bad. I carried that guilt for many years, until we were able to build some bridges and become friends.' **Sarah**

Shame, on the other hand, is a painful feeling arising from the consciousness of something dishonourable, improper, ridiculous, etc, done by oneself or another. In other words, guilt relates to others, shame to ourselves. Given Burgo's distinction, it's clear why divorce, which involves two people, can result in both, and many of the men and women I have spoken to mention shame. They sense people whispering 'can't keep her man', 'reckon he couldn't satisfy her' or similar. I remember going to our local supermarket, where I often used to bump into people I knew, and burning crimson with shame. I felt as though a neon sign above my head blazed 'my husband left me'. People often say that the shame is the other person's if they have behaved badly but I know that it is easy to internalise as part and parcel of a general feeling of having failed.

TIP: Most of us have an internal moral compass. Try to stay true to yourself. In this way, you are more likely to be able to hold your head high.

> 'I used to feel a lot of shame about ending my marriage. Eventually I learned to handle these emotions differently. Now I ask myself "Why does it seem so important what people think of me?" This has helped me to manage my inner critic.' **Sue**

FACT: Sometimes bad things happen to good people. Falling out of love (whether you or your partner or both) may just be one of those things. It does not mean you are a bad person. And there need be no shame in it.

2.8 Loss of confidence

'I'd start something and immediately get distracted, switch my attention and get distracted again. Lots of plates spinning, and most of them fell. I felt so useless.' **Maria**

Our marriage vows often contain the words to the effect of 'till death do us part', and most of us enter into marriage thinking we will spend the rest of our lives together. Around the world we are brought up on stories of happy ever after in fairy tales and movies. So it's no surprise that the end of a relationship can feel like a personal failure. In addition, if you were being deceived (infidelity, gambling, whatever) you may feel so completely undermined that it is difficult to believe you can do anything well. Your emotions are all over the place, and suddenly you are being asked to make big decisions without the very person you would normally turn to for support. It's easy to feel overwhelmed and not up to the task. You may want to bury your head in the sand and hope it will all go away. However, **you have to do this, and you can.** Read on for support through the stages of divorce, and sources of further help and, gradually, your self-esteem will grow.

41

2.9 Impact on children

In an ideal world, both parents would sit down together and explain to the children (of whatever age) that Mum and Dad are going to be living separately, but that they will still be Mum and Dad and still love them.

This happens rarely, unfortunately. And even if it does, the children are likely to have many worries about the future, about hurting their parents and even about whether this is in some way their fault. We will come back to the children in later chapters but it is worth mentioning here that while you may be suffering any of the emotional and physical symptoms described above, your children may also. Much of what causes these is uncertainty and lack of control, and this is probably even more true for children than for you.

> *'There is still fallout for the kids – they have their own issues, affecting them in different ways – but I'm glad to have got them out. An abusive relationship was the crappiest situation for them to be growing up in, and I didn't want them thinking that was how a marriage should be. So, if for no other reason, it was worth leaving for their sakes.'* **Maggie**

2.10 Further impact

It is likely that many, many things about your life are going to change: where you live, whether you work, your social life, what you do for holidays, maybe even your name… Some of these will be dealt with in sections about the legal and practical sides of divorce, others in the final chapter about emerging from divorce and moving on with your new life. Meanwhile, let's move on: dealing with the practicalities of a split can help reduce anxiety.

> *'I wish I could tell you it gets better, but… it doesn't get better.* ***You*** *get better.'* **Joan Rivers**

3. 'V' IS FOR VACATING THE RELATIONSHIP
WHAT NEEDS TO BE DONE TO
DISENTANGLE YOUR LIVES

Extricating yourself from a relationship of long standing is bound to be complicated. If you were married, and if you have children, even more so.

Quite apart from the legal aspects, to which we will turn later, and the emotional impact discussed in the previous chapter, there are dozens of practical considerations, large and small. Probably at least one of you is going to have to move house, possibly both. There may be issues around where the children live or how they split their time. What are you going to do for money? Who pays which bills? Will you change your name? Your childcare arrangements? Think of all the people you need to tell, officially (council, benefits people, schools etc) and unofficially. Not to mention the millions of questions like: what about the holiday that's already paid for, and who's going to have The Rolling Stones' *Sticky Fingers* CD?

For each of these, the potential for argument and upset is vast (again, especially when there are children to consider as well). Cumulatively this would represent quite a mountain to climb when you are working at full strength. But if your world has just been rocked and you are suffering from the emotional onslaught described in the previous chapter, you may well feel completely at sea. If your partner was the breadwinner and is no longer contributing to your costs, or those of your children or jointly owned home (sadly this is not uncommon, and it happened to me) there is the additional stress of worrying about how to manage financially. I lived for a long time with the threat of eviction, which does little to help you feel on top of things!

> *'On Christmas Eve, the day after a bruising nine-hour meeting with my ex and our lawyers, I went to hospital for 'pre-surgery'. Normally my ex would have accompanied me. I went alone, was faced with a barrage of questions and was floored by the barked "Next of kin?" I had not prepared for this. My children were too young to be given the responsibility. I had not asked any friends. In the end the nurse left it blank, which was another worry.'* **Eliza**

If you're anything like I was, not knowing where to start may stop you from doing anything as thoughts whirr round your mind, vying for attention. Remember, you don't have to tackle it all at once. It's like the watermelon that gets eaten in slices. So, let's break it down. In this chapter we look – broad brush – at the main areas that you will need to tackle in the immediate aftermath of your separation: children, housing, and money, to give you an overview of what to expect. Though so as not to overwhelm you, we've assumed matters are not too acrimonious at this point. Should you find relations get sticky and, sadly, they sometimes do, you will find Chapter 6 of help, I hope.

Let's kick off with some general advice.

TIP: Try to make lists. I tended to send myself emails from my phone, always replying to the last, as and when things occurred to me. This meant I had everything in one place, rather than on random scraps of paper.

The problem you may then face (I did) was that the list becomes overwhelmingly long and unwieldy. Just the thought of trying to sort it or prioritise was sometimes more than I could bear. Alternatively, you could do what Sarah suggests:

'I've a wipe-board and a set of coloured markers. Each colour represents an area of my life – red relates to work, blue to caring for my elderly mother, purple to health and so on. When I was going through my divorce there was a colour for that too. I like to tick things off when I've done them as it gives me a sense of achievement.'

And if that still sounds too much…

TIP: Remember how we talked about taking your separation one step at a time? Try to focus on doing just *one thing* each day. Most of it can wait, and you might find that you benefit from a less immediate and reactive response.

'Sometimes it was all I could do to put the washing on, and I only managed that because the children needed clean school uniform.' **Eliza**

3.1 Getting help

Tackling all the admin when you may still be in shock or depressed, and when your children are also needy and anxious, may be too much to take on alone. It can be difficult to ask for help but do try to enlist someone – or, better still, several people. I remember with gratitude the friends who produced their Form E (see Chapter 5) to help me with mine.

TIP: If you can, ask for something specific (a casserole you can shove in the oven, picking your kids up from football, a hand with packing for a house move), then friends who are not sure how they can help will be glad to step up.

'My mate had to say "Len, it's not a sign of weakness to ask for support, don't be embarrassed" as I felt so uncomfortable initially.' **Len**

3.1i Friends and family

'When I left my husband, my mother was a great source of support. Whereas some friends and more distant relatives were judgmental as I was the one who initiated the split, I always knew Mum was on my side. She urged me to be generous when making a settlement, as she believed going to court would cost me dearer emotionally and financially in the long run.' **Sarah**

Good friends and wise family members can help you, and if you know someone who is practical, or is a lawyer or an accountant, better still. Some close friends and family members might not find it easy to be objective, but broadly speaking it is easier to deal with tasks when they are not your own. Get someone level-headed to sit down with you and together you'll make much lighter work of admin that can panic you when you are alone.

'I couldn't face the task of filling all the forms. Part of me thought that if I ignored it, it wouldn't happen. A friend sat with me and gently forced me to begin. It became easier, once we'd started.' **Lisa**

TIP: Someone to take your children somewhere for a treat or a playdate while you get things done can be good for all of you.

'Allowing people to help you is so important – they may not do it your way, but so what? If they can get two things off your 'to-do' list of a hundred, then does the way they set about it really matter?' **Sue**

3.1ii Professional help

You may decide to enlist professional support, if you can afford it. We are not talking here about lawyers for the legal side, but other (possibly cheaper) people you might like to have on your team.

Divorce Coaches[16]
Yes, these are a thing! They help you navigate your way through what can appear to be an overwhelming minefield during a crisis. It may sound like a mad extravagance, but using a divorce coach might possibly end up saving you money. They are generally cheaper than lawyers and can prevent you from spending an unnecessary fortune having the same conversations at a higher hourly rate.

> FACT: *Anyone* can set themselves up as a divorce coach or PA and they are not (necessarily) trained in the law or in counselling, so do ask for personal recommendations and check that their credentials are genuine.

Also, note that you may still need a lawyer; the legal aspects and advice on choosing representation are discussed in Chapter 5.

Mediation
While a divorce coach could help *you* with various aspects of your divorce (depending on their background and your need), a mediator is there to help you agree things *with your ex*, if that is proving hard

otherwise. With hurt, recriminations and emotions running high, this is often the case. A mediator can help you to have civilized discussions (usually regarding children or finances) and work towards consensus at any stage during the separation or after. Mediators are sometimes, but not always, trained lawyers. You can find a mediator via the sources on p.185, and for more information about different types of lawyers, see Chapter 5.

3.1iii Free help and support online

There are other, free, sources of help, whether it's a quick question about how to fill a court form, or a virtual shoulder to cry on.

- **Sorting Out Separation**[17] is a government site offering authoritative advice and further sources of help in clear, concise English
- **Gingerbread**[18] and other organisations listed under the section on children in Chapter 4 also provide lots of help with separation
- Many people, including me, have found **Wikivorce**[19] to be a lifesaver
- There are further sources of support for specific situations, see p.185.

TIP: And don't forget the friendly bunch in our own Making Peace with Divorce Facebook group[20].

3.2   The Marital Pot

When it comes to disentangling, the two knottiest areas tend to involve joint finances and offspring. I'll start with fiscal matters, as pretty much all separating couples will want to sever their finances as much as possible, whereas not all couples have children.

Two Myths:

1. It is a common misconception that who owned what prior to marriage makes a difference. Generally speaking, it does not.

2. Another mistaken belief is that it matters a jot whose name things are in. Generally speaking, it does not.

> FACT: If you are legally married, then **everything either of you owns is usually deemed to be in the 'marital pot' for division.**[21]

This includes your home. Whether it was originally yours or your ex's, whether your name is on the mortgage or not, whether your ex ever paid towards it. In most cases (excluding for example very short marriages[22]) everything that one or other of you owns, if you are married, is regarded as jointly owned by you as a couple. Same with liabilities such as a mortgage or credit card debt.

TIP: Though assets are jointly owned, if your home is in the sole name of your ex it's a good idea to register marital rights to prevent it being sold or re-mortgaged without your permission – if this did happen it would be taken into account in divorce, but prevention is better than cure.

Similarly, who actually earned the money is not normally relevant. If, as a couple, it was decided that one of you should give up a career (to look after children or elderly parents, or to retrain, or for health reasons) the assumption that both should be treated fairly and end up similarly well or poorly off still stands. The contribution of the stay at home parent, whose support allowed the other to travel or work long hours to further his or her career is deemed equal in law.

> *'I worked my fingers to the bone to afford our home while she stayed home with the kids. Now she's been sleeping with some other bloke and *I* have to move out!'* **Nick**

> *'This was my flat before we even met, and he never contributed to the mortgage the whole time he lived here, so I don't see why he should get anything from it.'* **Aditi**

This applies not only to any property you own, but also to any inheritance or gift, as well as your businesses[23].

TIP: Remember to allow time for the valuation of properties and businesses, especially as this could prove contentious and involve some back and forth.

> FACT: At the time of writing, pre-nuptial and post-nuptial agreements are not legally binding in the UK. We have seen them taken into account by judges in recent years, but the court still has the discretion to waive agreements if they are deemed to be unfair to either party or to the children.

3.2i Your Home

Probably you will live apart, although some couples, for one reason or another, manage to continue to live under one roof. Luckily I was never tested in this regard as the first I knew of our separation was the disappearance of my ex, but some people do manage, whether for the children, for financial reasons, or because they get on fine as flatmates.

'Things are amicable and I have moved into the spare room. But whenever I hear the hairdryer, I know she is off out with him.' **Lee**

TIP: Get used to the fact that you are going to have to make economies, even if you feel 'it's not fair!' and 'it's not my fault!'

Naturally the wealthier you are as a couple, the greater flexibility you have regarding who lives where. If you own a property, this is likely to be your largest asset, and may well have to be sold to provide for two households. A court will divide any equity in the property on the basis of need. Another principle of the court is that **both partners should be left with comparable standards of living to one another.**

> FACT: There is no formula in the UK setting out how assets are to be split on divorce. While there is a basic assumption of 50:50, there are many factors to be taken into account, such as earning capacity, in order to reach a settlement which meets the needs of the couple, and especially any children, and seems fair.

3.2ii Income

Your finances are likely to become more straightened when you separate. If there isn't much to go around, you may want to (and have to: the courts would expect it) maximize your income. If you have young children and have not been working outside the home, you may well now have to do so. Maybe retrain for a new career if you have had many years out of the workforce. If you were working part time, you might have to increase your hours. You may also find you now qualify for benefits you did not previously claim.

TIP: Go to the benefit calculator on www.gov.uk to see what you could be entitled to. The site also has information about how to claim.

'I'd never been on benefits before and was ashamed to think I was sponging off the state. But I don't know where I would have been without them, as my ex cut off all money and I had none of my own.' **Jian**

3.2iii Financial disassociation

If you had joint bank accounts or a mortgage together, your credit rating will be affected by your ex; indeed it may be even if you only shared an address. It's a good idea to apply for financial disassociation, which you will have to do with all three of the credit reference agencies: Experian, Equifax and Callcredit[24]. As a stay at home mum, there was little I could do when my ex stopped paying the mortgage; as it was in both our names this affects me still, but I have filled in the relevant forms to try to counter the fact that he went on using our address for years when applying for loans.

'The reason I liken it to an STI[25] is that if your relationship breaks down, separating or divorcing doesn't make the linkage go away – problems can linger long after.' **Martin Lewis, MoneySavingExpert**

3.3 Other legalities

3.3i Your name

Some people (usually, but not only women) who took on their partner's name are keen to lose the association; others see no need. This is a very individual choice and may be affected by many things, including whether you have small children.

> *'I have used my married name longer than any other. My ex managed to destroy our family but he is not going to destroy who I am now, and he can't take away my name.'* **Charlie**

I have heard of women, on divorce, choosing neither the name of their former husband, nor that of their father, and going for something altogether different which they think suits them better, and why not? Changing your name by deed poll is a relatively straightforward thing but don't forget the hassle of updating all your records with banks, doctors, retailers etc.

> FACT: You can legally call yourself whatever you want, as long as there is no intent to defraud.

> *'You changed your name from Brown to Jones*
> *And mine from Brown to Blue.'* **Elvis Costello**

3.3ii Your Will

> FACT: A separation of no matter how long has no legal effect on a will: if you are still legally married or in a civil partnership, your will stands.

If there is no will[26]: your estate (largely) passes to your spouse[27]. If you want to ensure your soon-to-be-ex doesn't inherit, or to make sure someone else (children, new partner) benefits in the event that you die, a new will could be a priority.

> 'After I found out my ex had been siphoning funds for years to pay for prostitutes, I moved quickly to make sure he wouldn't get a penny from me if I went under a bus, and left my money to cancer research.' **Basia**

FACT: It is not the case, as is often supposed, that your will is void on divorce.

If your ex was named in your will: after divorce it's as though he or she is dead. Any provisions which benefit your ex are revoked. If no other beneficiaries are named, your estate will be distributed in accordance with the rules of intestacy, so if you want anything different, make a new will.

TIP: You do not need to get a solicitor to draw up a will.

You can buy kits from many large high street stationers (such as WH Smith or Rymans), or just Google what is required. Make sure you get the document witnessed and make it easy to find. (However, be aware that lawyers make a lot of money sorting out the messes left by DIY wills!) I did my own for the years between my ex leaving and decree absolute, then found a local solicitor (through one of the cut price schemes to encourage the making of wills) after I was divorced.

TIP: See MoneySavingExpert for ways to save money on making a will.

3.3iii Lasting power of attorney

If you are single (and if not!), think about making lasting powers of attorney so that in the event that you are incapacitated, someone can manage your affairs or make decisions about your health. You can choose more than one and specify whether they have to make decisions jointly, which may help relieve some anxiety you might have about entrusting one individual.

> *'I was advised about this when I got my will drawn up – it would not have occurred to me – but I chose a couple of friends for the financial decisions and an adult child for health.'* **Sharma**

Note: this is not just if you are old, frail or dying! Any one of us could find ourselves in hospital, and we would want to make sure someone else could access our money to pay our bills.

TIP: The UK Government site[28] **has information about lasting power of attorney.**

3.3iv Next of kin

If you have to choose someone to look after you or be notified in any emergency you may not have much time to think about it. You might want different friends or family members depending on the nature of the emergency, but it's worth some consideration in advance.

TIP: Mark the contact details of your nearest or dearest in your phone eg 'ICE – Joe Smith, son', 'ICE – Jane Brown, neighbour', so people know who to look for In Case of Emergency. This is a worldwide initiative promoted by emergency services.

3.3v Notifying authorities

There is a seemingly endless list of people who need or want to know about your changed circumstances:

- Banks – if you had any joint bank accounts
- The tax office – HMRC – should be notified of any relationship or family changes
- Your GP
- The council (if you are now the only adult living in the property you could be eligible for a discount)
- Post Office – redirect post if you are moving
- Utilities – if the person named on the bill has changed (you may need them to be in your name as proof of address)
- Insurance – not only because they like to know everything about you, but perhaps the value of your contents has changed (maybe your ex has taken her jewellery or computer) or your car has moved to a new address, or you want to change life insurance
- Your children's schools

If you are changing your name, the list is longer still!

'My husband had always dealt with 'manly' things like cars and finance. The first time I had to renew my car insurance, I discovered I had always been the 'named driver', so, after 25 years of blameless driving, he retained the 'no claims bonus' and my premiums shot up.' **Pia**

3.5 Children

Last, but by no means least, of all the issues that need to be sorted out in the wake of a separation between parents, far and away the biggest priority is the children. I've left it till last not because it isn't important, but because for those who *don't* have children, the rest of this chapter isn't relevant, so child-free readers, please do skip this and head to Chapter 4. But for those with offspring, there's a lot to sort.

3.5i Managing the separation well for your children

As we mentioned in Chapter 2, **ideally your children should maintain as much contact as possible with both parents and be given as much love and reassurance as you can *both* offer.**

When my husband left, although I was heartbroken on my own account, I was completely devastated at the thought of the effect our separation would have on my children. You will no doubt have heard horror stories about how badly children from 'broken families' perform; that they have behavioural issues, do less well in school and so on. I do not want to minimize the hurt and long-term effects on children – research suggests your child's education is likely to be impacted by divorce, which can also cause difficulties in adult relationships later on.

Naturally you will be concerned for your own offspring and you *do* have to take care to reduce anxiety for them as much as possible, but as friends reassured me: '*children are resilient*'. Recent research[29] by the family law organization Resolution reveals that whilst children dislike being caught in the middle of arguing parents and can feel side lined in the decision-making process, in the long term they can come to see their parents' divorce as a good thing. So **it seems fair to conclude that it's *parental conflict* that has the most damaging effect on children, not divorce itself.** And we all know people who have survived into well-adjusted adulthood despite having divorced parents – you may be one yourself!

> '*Our marriage was not good for years and I hung on for the sake of the kids. But then I met someone. I was surprised when the eldest said she was pleased for me, until she explained she was sick of me and her mum arguing and was relieved we were finally separating.*' **Matthew**

As a counsellor told me: 'a good divorce is better for children than a bad marriage'. These days I can see that she was right. So now that your marriage (or cohabitation) is over, **try to give your children and yourselves a good divorce.**

FACT[30]: Over half of couples divorcing in the UK in 2007 had at least one child aged under 16. This meant that there were over 110,000 children who were aged under 16 when their parents divorced. 20% of these children were under five years old. However, many more children go through parental separation each year that are not included in figures like this, as their parents were not married.

'It's a shame my partner and I had to split up as we had a small child, but now I look back, I think that by and large we've managed the separation well for him. My ex and I often don't see eye to eye and I've had to bite my tongue a lot over the years and have found it hard to meet her demands financially, but we've both been hands on all through his childhood. Cal is nearly 19 and a great kid. I'm proud of him.' **Len**

TIP: Remember that though they have their own concerns, children take their cue from you. By and large, if you cope, they will.

And, as Len proves, in spite of ongoing tension between the adults involved, a good divorce for children can still be achieved.

3.5ii Housing children

If you have kids, avoiding disruption for them if possible will be the priority of the courts. Therefore it is likely that the parent with the majority of childcare will stay in the family home if this is an affordable option. That way they can continue at their existing schools, live near their friends etc.

TIP: Think hard about your needs, and the children's, and be reasonable. How many bedrooms do you need? How near to school/work/family?

Sometimes, to allow one partner to stay in the family home with children, the other takes a greater share of other assets. If this is not feasible, sometimes the partner moving out retains a share in the property. This arrangement, known as a Mesher Order, commonly has a fixed end (eg the youngest child finishing school or the resident partner remarrying) at which point the home is sold with each parent receiving an agreed share of the equity.

3.5iii A Parenting Plan

Even if there are no disputes regarding the children and you are arranging your separation without going to court, a Parenting Plan is a good idea. It will help to clarify your thinking and to ensure that arrangements are in the best interests of the children, and workable. You will both then know where you stand. Templates for these are easy to find online (see below).

The first thing to consider is how your children can best maintain contact with both parents.

- What will be the living arrangements?
- Will they have one home or two?
- Where will they spend their weekends?
- Will you alternate?
- What about birthdays, Christmas, holidays?
- Who will do the driving back and forth and where will the handover take place?

Then there are further considerations, for example:

- Education (where they go to school, rules about homework)
- Music practice and after school clubs
- Pocket money
- Screen time
- Religion (if the two of you have differing views)
- Healthcare (there may be specifics to do with a health condition)
- Time spent with other family members such as grandparents

Factors influencing the plan can include:

- Age (eg if still breastfeeding)
- Where both parents are living (eg for travel to school)
- Money – is there enough for both parents to have enough bedrooms?
- Childcare arrangements eg if both parents work, it may not be practical to have two homes as far as nursery, childminder or nanny is concerned
- New partners (if any) and any children of theirs
- Safeguarding issues, ie if there are concerns about the safety of children with one or other parent (abuse, substance misuse)
- Children's preference (if they are old enough)

It's best for you and your ex to consider these issues and come to a formal or informal agreement or parenting plan. If you can't decide, a judge will. This is likely to be more stressful and expensive and to cause bad feelings all round, so do try to sort things amongst yourselves. (And if it does come to court, the judge will expect you to have worked on a parenting plan.)

TIP: Take a look at some of the examples you can find online, to help ensure you cover all aspects relevant to your own family.

'At first we just muddled along; after a while it began to grate that my ex would change plans and expect us all to work around her at the last minute, so we drew up a plan and now we all know where we stand. I still get annoyed by her but I am better able to say no.' **Khalid**

There is help available to you to prevent the situation escalating and going to court, much of it available through Cafcass, the Children and Family Court Advisory and Support Service.

- **Example Parenting Plan**[31] **and guidance at Cafcass**. There is lots of good information here.
- **Free helpline for separated parents** – Cafcass is piloting this in some parts of the country.
- **Child Maintenance Options**[32] – useful information and a free helpline.
- **SPIP**[33] – Separated Parents Information Programme – these are courses to help you to put your children first during separation. They are sometimes free and, while it's best if both parents attend, you won't be in the same group as your ex.
- **Mediation** – there is a fee for mediation (though legal aid may be available). To find your nearest family mediator visit familymediationhelpline.co.uk/find-service.php
- **Parent Connection**, 'parenting after parting' at theparentconnection.org.uk has various free resources to support you.

- **Gingerbread.org.uk** provide expert advice, practical support and campaign for single parents, including those going through separation, and have lots of useful information online such as FAQ about contact arrangements.

TIP: If you can, work on this together and involve the children where appropriate without burdening them.

'At first my children used to go out to dinner once a week with their dad. Then my son started not wanting to go. It took us a while to get to the bottom of it. He didn't mind seeing his father, but he didn't want it to be in a restaurant, or with his sisters.' **Kirsten**

TIP: Many counsellors specialise in seeing children or families to help resolve issues between family members.

There are family therapy centres, as well as individual counsellors that you will find through the sources of counsellors listed at the end of this book. They are very experienced in dealing with separation and children, and can help you to come to an agreement as a family, bearing in mind the changes that are taking place.

If you can't sort this, or discussions break down, you may need recourse to the courts. On the other hand, if relations between you are amicable, or sometimes for other reasons (like the disappearance of one parent) you may not need any such thing. I never had one. I was a stay-at-home mum and my ex travelled a lot for work. There was never any question that they would not live with me and, even when I could hardly think straight, I was 100 per cent clear that I wanted to do everything I could to facilitate good relations between the children and their father.

3.5iv Money for children

One of the stresses facing separating parents is the cost of maintaining two households instead of one. Obviously for all but the very wealthy this is likely to have a material effect of the standard of living of everyone concerned. How will you afford to provide for yourselves and your children, and how will the costs be divided?

Again it helps if you can agree between yourselves how the costs of your **children** will be met. Usually, the parent with the greater earnings (whether mother or father) will be expected to contribute more to these costs. If one parent has been at home looking after the children while you were both together, and the other supported the family financially, this can expect to continue, at least while the children are very young, if it is at all affordable. A 'family based arrangement' is a private way to sort out child maintenance. Child maintenance is usually paid by the parent who does not have main day-to-day care of the children to the 'receiving' parent, who does.

'I can't go out to work; our child has special needs and I gave up work to care for her, so I rely on maintenance from my ex and benefits.' **Anne**

As it says on the helpful Child Maintenance Options[34] site (a free service provided on behalf of the Department of Work and Pensions): all parents are financially responsible for their children. If a parent lives apart from their child, financial responsibility usually means paying maintenance to the parent with the main day-to-day care of the child.

FACT: All parents are financially responsible for their children even if they:

- Don't live with the child's other parent
- Aren't named on the birth certificate
- Don't have any formal parental responsibility

TIP: Try to keep emotion out of this. Stick to hard facts about costs.

If you can't reach an agreement between you, you have recourse to the courts and to the Child Maintenance Service (CMS). This replaces the Child Support Agency (CSA) that you may have heard of. We will return to the issue of child maintenance in later chapters, but first, let's look at the issue of communication, which can make such a big difference to the way your separation pans out, as well as to the way you feel about it.

4. 'O' IS FOR OTHER PEOPLE
COMMUNICATING WITH YOUR EX,
YOUR CHILDREN, YOUR FAMILY AND FRIENDS

When you are splitting up, it can be easy for your emotions to get the better of you. Suddenly, other than in the most amicable 'we're going our separate ways but are still best friends' scenario, the very person who used to have your corner, does not. In many cases, even if there hasn't been deception, even if neither of you has dumped the other, you will now be adversaries. It all seems confusing, hurtful and *wrong*. Whilst separation may be more common these days, nonetheless it goes against a notion we've been brought up on, of 'happy endings' that feature in mythology and popular culture around the world. You may well want to scream and shout, tear your hair out, tell your story to everyone you meet, or hide away and tell nobody. It's likely there will be times when you want to throttle your ex, especially if they have hurt you. We've all heard the stories of revenge, of sleeves being cut off suits etc. (My favourite tale of this type concerns a woman who quietly had all her ex's suits taken in by just half an inch...) Lord knows it can be tempting but this is not a way to behave!

'Aristocrat who wrecked house to spite ex-wife is facing prison.'
***Evening Standard* headline, 18 July 2017**

TIP: For your own peace of mind; to model behaviour for your children, if you have them; and to find the best resolution, try to deal with this situation in a way that is civilised and rational.

I'm not advocating that you suppress all your emotions – far from it. Just that you find a safe space to express them, to keep things as clean as you can. It's wise to try your best not to make things worse.

4.1 Communicating with your ex

In most cases, when one of you calls time on a relationship, there is going to be hurt, bewilderment, resentment and anger. If you have been left, you may feel an overwhelming urge to persuade your ex that he or she is making a mistake (I did), or to understand why he or she is behaving this way (me too). Whether it's face-to-face or phone calls, emails or texts, you may think that if you explain your side, or make promises, you can get things back the way they were. Generally speaking, your ex does not want to know. Or maybe your ex *will* engage and communications will spiral out of control. You won't be able to think of anything else but what your ex said, and what it meant, and how you responded, and what you will say next time, and…

However, in the end, it will almost certainly not bring your ex round, and will only draw the whole thing out longer. For this reason, many people recommend the *No Contact Rule.*

4.1i No Contact Rule

Essentially, the idea is to go cold turkey, to break the habit or addiction of communication with your former partner. If you communicate, the theory goes, it feeds the neediness, escalates the argument, and prolongs the hurt. Some talk about a minimum of 60 days of no contact and many people swear by it.

'I did 60 days no contact and though it was tough, it really was the most important thing I did to accelerate my healing. Afterwards, I never went back to contacting him or wanting to know what he was doing. The pain of separation was still there but there was no more salt going into open wounds.' **Shula**

'For anyone pondering whether cutting contact works, please believe me it does. It is very hard but nothing works better for achieving some emotional distance.' **Sam**

'I don't know about you, but any communication I had with my ex when we were going through divorce left me feeling worse than before any communication started. It was pointless.' **Ravi**

'It means no contact other than what is required for civilised living (so you do say hello if you pass in the street). It means no talking, messaging, emailing, no looking at their social media. It's not for their benefit but to enable you to get some clarity, to allow your emotions to calm and get some control over them.' **Poppy**

'Invest in a pair of boxing gloves. Put them on whenever you feel tempted to text.' **Howard**

TIP: Some people find it cathartic to write a letter to their ex, maybe on beautiful paper, then put it in a drawer, or ritualistically burn it.

Naturally, there may be times that you need to communicate, most obviously if you have young children together.

TIP: For making arrangements regarding the children, if possible stick to business-like, factual texts.

Even where there are only adult children, or none, you may need to communicate over practical or legal matters. The *No Contact Rule* would have this be as simple and business-like as possible.

4.1ii Language

Avoid emotive language in order not to lose control during interactions with your ex. This will make it easier to distance yourself and prevent an argument. Therefore, in conversations or in writing, avoid referring to the past (blame, who said what or who started it) and stick to the issues that need to be resolved. Try to keep any edge out of your voice, even if you believe yourself the innocent victim. (I didn't say it was easy!)

> *'After my 60 days no contact, I employed business-like contact only. If he asked, "what have you been up to?" I'd say, "I've been busy thanks". Then I'd just be quiet. I had a discipline of answering his questions with two or three words. I'd never ask him anything. I refused to engage on anything apart from the divorce.'* **Cindy**

TIP: Focus on present facts; do not refer to emotions or the past.

We've already mentioned avoiding the use of should/shouldn't/always/never. 'Still it can be hard not to get caught up in blaming and shaming the other person,' says Sarah. 'All too easily we can slip into storytelling, or justifying, so keep it short and simple.' An example may help to explain.

EXAMPLE 1

> *'Please pick the children up at the agreed time.'*

EXAMPLE 2

'You didn't pick up the children on Friday! Think how that made them feel! You are always so unreliable! You've let your children down again. I don't care if you got caught up in traffic – next time be there on the dot, or else. If this is the way you're going to behave, I won't let you see them at all because it upsets them too much.'

Can you see how the second example is full of judgement? It also questions the other person's integrity, discounts their explanation and is threatening – past and future are both drawn in. Notice how many more words it takes to be angry.

You also might want to look into Nonviolent Communication[35] for help with using appropriate strategies for resolution.

TIP: If your ex was abusive, communications and co-parenting can be much more challenging. See divorcedmoms.com[36] for help.

I've seen advice that you allow your lawyer to communicate on your behalf, such as this:

'Your attorney is your advocate, and he or she can communicate effectively on your behalf without emotion clouding his or her judgment. Your attorney may also assist you with getting your needs met without having to go through your spouse.' **Raleigh Divorce Attorney**

They have a point, especially during negotiations, but, really, especially if you have children together, you can't hide behind your lawyer forever. (Quite apart from the cost!) Give some thought to how you communicate with the person who was your nearest and dearest, and try to make it work.

4.1iii Responding

Take your time. During my marriage I used to be very reactive and would often fire off immediate replies to texts. I stopped that. (Being on a three year Alexander Technique course – the Technique is all about putting a little space between stimulus and reaction – certainly helped!)

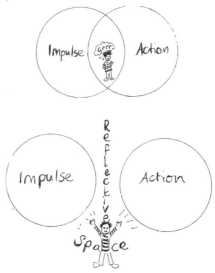

'I have a terrible temper, but if you can recognise yourself in the second example above (and I do!), the ancient wisdom suggesting you "count to ten" can be very helpful,' agrees Sarah. 'Though if you're very wound up, ten seconds is rarely long enough.'

TIP: Make it a rule never to reply to anything straight away. 'Sleep on it' is a good rule of thumb.

Once I engaged a lawyer, I created a new email address for her to use and did not have it forward to my normal email or phone. That way I knew I would not be interrupted and could wait until I was ready, at my desk with a cup of tea, to log in and receive the next hammer blow. This is likely to be more secure as well, if you fear your ex has access to your accounts and passwords (which you really should change immediately if you have not done so!).

TIP: Create a dedicated email for all your lawyer's divorce correspondence.

That is all very well for your lawyer but what about your ex, who has your contact details? Some people block their exes and you may want to do that for phone calls, texts and emails. If, however, you have children who spend time with your ex, you'll need to be contactable. What I did was change the name of my ex in my contacts. I know other people have done this with rude or amusing names and photos, ringtones of ducks quacking or whatever. One friend, whose husband was conscious of his stature, used a photo of Napoleon. I simply changed the name of mine to The Respondent, which helped me to keep my distance.

TIP: Change your ex's details in your contacts to something which makes you laugh (or at least doesn't make you cry!)

4.1iv Social media

With all of us so connected these days by social media, there is an extra layer to disentangling ourselves. It's not just the ex him- or herself either; there are all the friends and family to consider.

Think about the degrees of separation you want for your ex and any mutual friends on Facebook. You may have to block your ex. If they are hassling you, it's very wise to do so. If not, a softer option is to unfriend them, or demote them to 'acquaintance'.

TIP: If relations are cordial, you can always explain via email that you wish your ex well but that you will be unfriending to protect yourself.

If you unfriend your ex, chances are you will still have other friends in common, so there is a risk of seeing stuff that may upset or enrage you in posts where your ex is tagged or has commented. Your ex may be getting remarried, or having a jolly time on holiday, and appear in their photos, or might comment on their posts. If this is the case, you can stop following mutual friends so their updates don't appear in your timeline, or go further and block your ex.

TIP: Remember, you can always reinstate people to their original status later.

'I'm not ready to see her being well-adjusted or having a good time, though I know it's petty of me. It just hurts too much to have that constant reminder.' **Alan**

TIP: Never post in your pyjamas. Or when you've had a drink.

You may also not feel comfortable with him or her (or your in-laws or former friends) seeing what *you* are up to. If you have kept them as FB friends, you can still prevent individuals from seeing your posts, if you like, by choosing 'friends except' from

the audience selector. Or you can add them to your 'restricted' list. That way you can still use the site.

'In order to feel like I still had my community, my safe place, I had to unfriend everyone with whom we overlapped. [...] And, I have told some people, "yes, I did unfriend you, but we can stay in touch in this other way." Friends, real friends, figure out ways to stay friends, either on or off Facebook.' **Jenny Kanevsky in *The Good Men Project*[37]**

TIP: If you need to vent, rather than post vitriol or misery (or gloating) on your own wall, stick to the more boundaried space of the closed Making Peace With Divorce group on Facebook.

TIP: It may be an idea to lay off social media altogether for a while.

It's not just Facebook, of course. My ex and I met at business school. We have a large number of mutual connections on LinkedIn, and are both likely to be on the guest lists for reunions and the like. So far, I just don't go. And then I steer clear of photos showing him sitting at champagne strewn tables surrounded by my peers because I know that when I see them I feel sick, or sad, or angry, which does nothing to help me. These feelings do diminish over time, so nowadays I am more dispassionate when I come across him online, but I do not feel the need to know what he is up to and I would advise others to resist any temptation to find out about their exes.

TIP: Try to avoid 'pain shopping' – where you go looking for your ex online, or wallowing in memories, and only end up being hurt.

Some people have a relationship status on their profiles in FB etc, and wonder about changing this, what people will think etc. My view is that you should be honest, but you don't have to share everything.

It goes without saying that you should refrain from venting in public, and that includes online. Remember: once it's out there, even if you delete your post, it may be too late. Once again, err on the side of sleeping on it and, ideally, say nothing.

4.1v Meeting

Until you have been in this position yourself it is hard to imagine how being in the same room as your ex can make you feel utterly wretched or completely enraged. Handovers, if you have small children, are often a point of conflict and upset, and can be confusing and unpleasant for the children to witness.

'Over the years everything would be running along smoothly, then there would be an explosion. It was often over money but we also argued about taking our son to and fro. She wanted me to have him more often and I understood her need to have a break, but she also needed me to earn money to pay maintenance. I'm self-employed so I was caught between a rock and a hard place. I'd get so frustrated, then I'd fly into a rage. I felt undermined in so many ways – by how she spoke to me, she didn't seem to respect my ability to look after my own son – and by how little she seemed to value me.' **Matt**

TIP: If logistics allow, it may help to ask a grandparent or friend to be there when the children are being picked up or dropped off.

'My ex used to come into the house every time he dropped off or picked up the children. Just having him over the threshold was too much and in the end I said so.' **Sal**

Similarly, rows can erupt on the doorstep if one of you drops by to pick up personal effects, so maybe agree to have stuff outside the door at a specified time.

'I'd come home to find he'd been round and helped himself from the fridge. He'd leave a mess in the kitchen, just as before. Whether he'd rummaged around elsewhere I don't know. I asked him to stop but he said it was still his house, too.' **Maria**

TIP: Even if your mortgage is still in both names, if one of you has moved out, he or she does not have the right to enter without permission. If you still live there, it may still be a joint asset, but it is now your home, where you have a right to privacy.

In some cases, meetings are inevitable. Mediation. Court. For me, the very thought of seeing him made me retch. I wish I could say I was able to be civil, but the only way I could cope at all was to blank him out altogether and focus on my breathing.

'I had two sessions of mediation. Hardest thing I've ever had to do, control my emotions in a room with a philanderer.' **Wendy**

In the early days, people will understand if you can't face meeting your ex. Further down the line, there may be graduations and weddings and funerals where you might have to be in some proximity to one another. So far I have not been able to countenance the notion. Not because we are no longer together, or because I want us to be (I don't) but because of the way he continues to behave towards me and – more importantly – my children. I aspire to be able to rise above it for their sakes.

And I am lucky. I live in London. Chances of our bumping into one another by chance are slim. If you live in a small town or village it is much harder. Maybe you even still work together. Lord knows, some couples, for family or financial reasons, continue to *live* together while going through a separation, even when things are not amicable, which must be incredibly hard. If this is your situation, you have my admiration and sympathy! There can be little escape or privacy, and the temptation to retaliate and hurt one another must have a terrible effect on the atmosphere. Try to be civil and treat your ex as a flat mate deserving of respect. If you are enjoying a new relationship, be tactful and don't rub your ex's face in it. Partners who have just been asked for a divorce will naturally find it hurtful if you start taking care over your appearance and staying out all hours, ecstatic while they are numb with grief.

Tips on interacting with your ex if you are the one who ended it, from Sarah:

- Respect his or her need for no contact. Don't initiate communication – leave the ball in your ex's court.
- Be kind. As we've said earlier in this book, a little empathy goes a long way.
- Avoid blame and shame.
- Be as materially generous as you can afford to be. If your generosity has its roots in guilt, so what? It may help you both feel a bit less awful, and we can't take money with us to the grave.
- Do not invite friends to take sides. Any friends that are more their friend than yours, leave well alone.
- Remember you are not the person to help them heal.
- And never say 'you should be over it by now'

'It is heartbreaking that he is moving on so fast. He only told the kids at the weekend, and he's out with her again tonight.' **Gillian**

4.2 Communicating with the children

If you have children, especially if they are still young and living at home, the question of divorce is many times more complex. There are extra people involved, who are liable to be hurt, and naturally you will want to protect them as much as possible.

TIP: Much as we want to shield our children from pain, they will suffer disappointments and heartbreak in their lives. Your behaviour at this point will model how they might handle sadness and misfortune in future.

> FACT: Many children, especially younger ones, continue to harbour hopes that their parents will get back together, no matter how unlikely or unpalatable this seems to you.

How you communicate with your children will obviously depend in part on their ages, as well as their temperaments, and yours. Below are some ideas and suggestions you may want to keep in mind.

4.2i Breaking the news

This is never going to be easy, but can be done in a way that makes your children feel supported.

TIP: It may seem too obvious to need doing but please *reassure the children that the split is not their fault.*

It can be difficult for children to blame their parents for bad things that happen in their lives because the parent is the source of correct behaviour, so often guilt is the default position of the child. And if they hear arguments that involve them (eg whose turn it is to pick them up or how to discipline them) they may conclude that *they* are the problem.

- Plan when and where to tell them: studies show that the memory of being told stays with children for a long time.
- If possible, both parents should be there and should present a united front.
- Tell them all together, rather than, for example, trying to shelter younger children, thus burdening older children with a secret.
- Don't try to reassure them by dismissing their fears, saying 'it will be OK'.
- Do reassure them that both parents still love them.
- Tell them as best you can how the separation will affect *their* lives, eg 'Mummy will not be living here, but she will still take you to football.'
- Reassure them about those things that will stay the same, eg 'You will still live in this house and go to the same school.'
- Don't feel that you have to have all the answers: admit if you don't know.
- Avoid giving too much information, and in particular any which paints either parent in a difficult light (eg mentioning affairs).
- Be prepared for any reaction (sadness, anger, indifference) and allow your children to express whatever they feel.
- Make it clear that they can talk to you at any time.
- Repeat what you have said, possibly many times, as it may take a while for it to sink in, and the children will need reassuring often.

'I remember my father sitting on the end of my bed and crying. I must have been 12 or 13. I couldn't cry too as I was focused on comforting him. So a lot of my emotions came out as rage and we had awful rows.' **Sarah**

'Ruby was being distraught in a way that was really acting out my distress. Ruby was too brave for her own good, really.' **Carol**

Teenagers

The suggestions above apply no matter what age your children are. For teenagers, you may also want to consider the following:

- Sometimes teenagers find eye contact difficult. For further discussions about the separation, car journeys or walks in the park can allow them to talk to you without feeling too exposed.
- Try to avoid questions that allow them to answer with a yes or no (you may still get a shrug or eyeroll!)
- Try not to badmouth your ex. Teenagers can be very judgemental.
- They probably find the thought of their parents having sex at all, never mind extra marital sex, absolutely sickening.
- In the wake of separation, sometimes children will try to care for their parents and take on too much responsibility, sometimes they will behave badly just when you may feel least able to cope, and they may veer from one to the other.

'Don't forget that your children will be going through grief, too, and that grief comes in waves. So just as you may lurch from fury to calm to upset and back again, so might they. I recall when my parents were splitting up, some days I couldn't give a fig and just happily got on with my life and my friendships, whilst on others it was all banging doors and cries of "I hate you!"' **Sarah**

'My mother told me one of the reasons she and my father were splitting up was because he was no good in bed. She even detailed why not! I was 15 at the time and I still cringe at the memory. Maybe she wanted me to understand her point of view but she lumbered me with a vision of my father's ineptitude that I can't shake many decades later.' **Minette**

TIP: Think of the long-term impact of your words. It might make you feel better to offload your grievances but your children are not the place for them. Confide in a broad-minded friend instead (or post on the Making Peace with Divorce group on Facebook).

'My children unfortunately grew up overnight when their dad left. I was in a terrible state and worry that I made things worse for them by leaning on them too much.' **Kirsten**

'It can be **so** tempting for parents to want children to understand their point of view, I get that, especially if they feel they have been treated badly,' says Sarah. 'Many of us are keen to convey just what a bastard/bitch our ex has been, and any offspring – who are around and who know the other person intimately – can seem the perfect place to vent spleen. For anyone wrestling with this, I'd suggest going back to the advice earlier in the chapter, where we explain how useful it can be to put space between the impulse and the action. I realise stopping mid-flow is tough. (Rest assured I am no paragon of virtue and have a horrific temper, when I let rip.) Nonetheless, whenever I hear friends of mine badmouthing their exes in front of their kids, I want to scream: "PLEASE DON'T DO THAT!" (Last time this happened, I suggested gently my friend and I talk about her ex later, when their son was in bed, and my friend said, "Oh, it's okay, my son knows all this already" – he was eleven years old, for goodness sake!).

'I'm aware that I feel strongly because it echoes my own past and *I hated it*. Yes, it helped me understand both my mother and my fathers' perspectives, but I loved them both and felt horribly torn. It's worth remembering that **whilst any child is half of one parent, they are also half of the other, and that child is not the one separating**. They are not on one side or the other (even if you sometimes feel they should be). They are **involved** intimately in divorce/separating enough already, by virtue of it happening. This means that unless there is an issue involving violence or abuse, adults in this situation will model the best behaviour if they try, *if they possibly can*, to dump somewhere else. Much better to tell a friend, a therapist, go or beat a pillow and to save confiding until the children are older (by which I mean no longer teenagers, say, and even then it may not be appropriate), and if you can't wait that long, then at least wait until morning, and sleep on it before spilling all the beans!'

Adult children

Let's not forget adult children. They have lives of their own and no longer live at home, so you may think they will be unaffected. In my research, I was surprised how often people were still very much shaken by the news even if they received it as grown ups themselves. Like many of us, they too questioned whether they had been deceived, and for how long, and wondered whether their past family life had been a sham. They could also be quite contemptuous of philandering or irresponsible parental behaviour.

> 'My parents divorced when I was 29 and even though I wasn't there and it caused very little disruption in my life, it shook me very much and I don't think I ever got over it.' **Lucy**

There are some children, particularly older ones, who think their parents' separation a good thing if there was tension in the family. All the same, remember that it can be upsetting.

Be truthful with your children, but also kind and gentle.

Listening

As well as talking to your children about what is going on, remember to *listen*. A good book (not divorce specific) is *'How to talk so children will listen, and listen so children will talk'*, by Adele Faber and Elaine Mazlish. To be a good listener, practice *reflective listening*. Do not pre-empt your child by finishing sentences or providing solutions. Instead, give your full attention, and feed back your understanding of what the child is saying, preferring silence to idle chatter.

'I was brought up with dysfunctional married parents who brawled and slept in separate rooms after my birth, blaming my presence. I fled at 18. Marriage trapped me in this 'prison' and did permanent emotional damage. Divorce by my parents would have released me. Let's not ever forget that divorce is sometimes better for a child. Better one parent than two bound together by a piece of paper.'
Cindy Cohen, letter to Prospect Magazine

4.2ii During the divorce and after

After the initial shock, going forward, some suggestions:

- Try to create new routines if necessary to replace old ones, so that there is some predictability in a time of anxiety, such as pizza night with Dad on a Friday or a stomp in the park at the weekend.
- Try to keep things normal (even though things may be far from normal for you!). For example, while a certain tolerance of reactive bad behaviour may be appropriate, do not indulge them too much or over-compensate for their loss with loads of treats.
- Be aware of how unsettling it can be for them to see you very upset.
- Tempting though it may be on both sides, try not to allow your children to fill any of the void left by your ex.
- Keep in mind, too, how they may be tempted to tell each of you what they think you want to hear.
- If you are the non-resident parent, too, remember to maintain consistency. If you see little of the children, and especially if you feel guilty or want to get into their good books, it can be tempting to try to 'make it up to them' or not enforce normal rules. Try not to spoil them with material things or an 'anything goes' attitude. And be reliable: you have left them once, don't disappoint them by changing plans or not showing up.

- If you are not able to spend as much time with your children as you used to, remember that you can write, phone, Skype etc. Why not make recordings of you reading bedtime stories that they can listen to any time they like?

TIP: the most precious thing you can give your children is your time and devoted attention.

It is important to do what you can to foster your child's good relations with both parents, for everyone's sake and especially the child's. Do not attempt to drive a wedge between them, which in any case will very likely rebound and make your child feel defensive.

'Time and again, when I was upset with my ex, I bit my tongue rather than offload onto our son, Jack. I didn't think it was fair on him – he was only a toddler when we split up. But it was very hard, as my ex would use him to manipulate me. If I couldn't afford to pay for something, she would say: "Alright then, but I'm going to tell Jack you don't want him to have it," and if I couldn't pick him up, she'd say: "Your dad doesn't want to come and collect you." So it's not surprising he used to side a lot with his mother. But Jack is grown up now and my ex can't threaten me with stopping him from seeing me. When I was caught in the middle it was awful – and it must have been horrible for him too – but now he's in control of how much we see each other it's a lot easier. I saw him every weekend while he was growing up and he still chooses to come here a lot. Recently Jack told my wife, Sally, that he realises he is very lucky compared to his friends. "I've got two parents who are both on my side," he said to her. I was so glad to hear he said this, and so was Sal. I think it's not so much that he's changed how he views his mum, as they're still very close. It's that he's old enough to see the situation as an adult. He has friends whose fathers don't seem to care that much, whereas I've been actively involved in Jack's life all along.' **Len**

If you share childcare, eg alternate weeks, do try to keep communications civil with your ex, as things are bound to come up when homework has been left behind or clothes have not been laundered. Your children will soon learn what is and is not allowed in each of their homes, but a certain level of consistency and cooperation will make everything run more smoothly. If their father only ever feeds them toast (or whatever), remember that you are separated parents now, and each can assert parental responsibility in their own time. And it's worth repeating, try not to make snide remarks or badmouth your ex in front of the children (always a good rule).

Problems with contact

It is heart breaking to witness the pain of your child being let down by the other parent and hard to know what to say. 'Daddy loves you, he's just very stressed at the moment' or 'Mummy just needs a bit of space to think' are hard for a child to understand, and start to wear thin when the missed dates or phone calls are many.

TIP: Sometimes it's best to admit you don't know why someone is behaving the way they are.

When my ex disappeared without warning or farewell, he was anxious to emphasise that he had left me but had not left our children. This was a line I repeated to them many times until one of them made the simple point that he had, in fact, left them, too. I stressed that it was not them he was unhappy with, just me.

If, as the non-resident parent, you are not seeing your child, whether by choice or because the child or resident parent is making it difficult, do keep trying. You want your child to know that you care. Do not assume, either, that the child is 'being poisoned' or 'used as a weapon'. Though this can happen, unfortunately, it is also often the case that the child is asserting his or her own unwillingness to condone the behaviour of one parent or another.

TIP: Send postcards and letters, cards and gifts.

Remember their birthdays and Christmas but, please, not just those days. Send little notes from time to time. Try to keep dialogue open, maybe with bits of your news as well as interest in theirs. Even if these are not acknowledged or reciprocated, keep it up. Try not to complain to them about lack of response.

> *'Decreasing contact between one parent and the child can lead to complete loss of contact over time, and children never get over the loss of a parent relationship – even as adults.'* **Divorcemag.com**

TIP: If relations between your children and the other parent deteriorate, keep calm, and keep a log of missed dates etc in case the issue has to go to court, but try not to *look* for fault.

4.2iii Counselling for kids

Though you make it clear you are available for your children to talk to about their feelings, they may not want to. You are too close, or hurting too much yourself, or they don't want to upset you. Try to make others available to them. Whether to a family member or friend to whom they are close, or a school counsellor, or a family therapist, encourage your child to speak to someone, *even if they insist that they are fine.*

TIP: Inform your child's school of the family circumstances. Staff will then be more understanding of any unusual behaviour.

Even if they seem OK, and even though divorce is commonplace now, studies show that experience of family break up (as well as experience of living in a high conflict household) can have lasting effects on a child's ability to form meaningful relationships when adult. They can become aggressive, hostile or violent; alternatively they can develop low self-esteem, anxiety or depression. If your child is coping well, it is still a good idea for them to have an outlet to discuss their feelings before they grow up and find their relationships affected by unresolved issues from this time.

Be aware, also, that while your child may not show signs of emotional distress, these feelings of anger or anxiety can also manifest in physical problems such as headaches, tummy ache, insomnia, fatigue etc.

4.2iv Introducing new partners

If you are in a new relationship, take it slowly when introducing the children. They will not like to think that Mummy or Daddy has been replaced so swiftly. Give them time to get used to the separation before throwing someone else into the mix.

TIP: Maybe a low-key meeting on neutral ground with some kind of escape, like a walk in the park, rather than a sit-down dinner in a restaurant.

Be prepared for them to be anything from hostile to ingratiating, irrespective how wonderful your new love is.

A word about merged families
If one of you has a new partner with children, or goes on to have children with a new partner, it is wise to tread carefully. While half and step siblings can be a source of great love and can enrich the lives of your children, it may be too much to expect this to happen overnight. There are almost bound to be jealousies and difficulties along the way as children see others as treading on their territory or taking attention from a parent. Much has been written on the subject of step and merged families, including an article by Sarah[38].

4.3   Communicating with others

It can be hard at first, knowing what or how much to say to people about what you are going through. Obviously it will depend on the circumstances and you will probably find a brief form of words that works.

- My marriage ended
- I'm separating from my partner
- I'm going through a divorce
- We are going our separate ways
- We are no longer together

These are less loaded or judgmental than 'my wife left me' or 'my husband was having an affair'.

'I remember being upset when my ex in the early days referred to "our separation" as though mutually agreed and civil, and I wanted to say, "We didn't separate – you scarpered without so much as a word to me or the children," but actually, not everyone needs to know that.' **Eliza**

Good friends will be there for you, will listen to the same old complaints and mop up tears. And some people just like the gossip and drama. But it really does get boring after a while, and, if you are a gusher rather than a bottler, you may still feel the need to express it all. A friend describes herself as feeling on a hamster wheel, endlessly going over the same thing, jumping straight back on after being distracted off it. I know just what she means! Rather than drive people away with the monotony of your unhappiness, indignation or new-found joy, if you really do keep wanting to go over and over, keep a journal. In these modern times you can do it online. Send it out there.

TIP: You may find it helpful to keep a journal or a blog.

I found this a great outlet – I started blogging in various places, including Wikivorce, which always has a supportive audience, and then switched to a separate blog under a pseudonym, which I enjoy writing to this day, about my changing life (and which was the basis of Sarah asking me to write this book). I rarely look at my statistics because, really, I don't write it for the people who follow or stumble upon it, but for myself. All the same it is a nice feeling to know that I am speaking to people in all the corners of the globe, and it makes me think that little bit harder about what I actually do think or feel, compared to writing in a book that remains private.

'Write hard and clear about what hurts.' **Ernest Hemingway**

Some of the people I met online have become close real-life friends, and with them I can still share those feelings that fellow divorcé(e)s will understand, both positive and negative.

And for everyone else, I no longer feel as though I have the words 'failed marriage' branded on my forehead, nor do I experience the need to regurgitate the whole gruesome story whenever I meet anyone. In fact, I wonder, when I see drop down menus on forms asking for status, whether I am 'divorced' or 'single' and what business it is of theirs anyway.

If you fall into the category of people who bottle things up, I would encourage you to find an outlet – a blog or counselling or both. Be wary though: as mentioned earlier, you may find it keeps you stuck in the pain of separation. It is helpful if it gives you insights that allow you to progress.

4.4 Communicating with yourself

We've touched on communication with your ex, with your children, if any, and with others in general. What is of paramount importance is how you speak *to yourself*.

> *'Be careful how you speak to yourself, because you are listening.'*
> **Seen on the internet**

People take divorce as a failure. 'My marriage failed' people say. I used to think this way.

Especially if the separation was thrust upon you, you are likely to take it badly. Early on, I frequently heard people advise me 'not to take it so personally'. I was stunned: how could I not? It was happening to me *personally*! I was being rejected, I was no good. Mea culpa. I must have been a bad wife. I went over and over the times I had been aggressive or sarcastic or whiny or sulky (of which there were many).

For a long time I thought my husband had left me because I was a bad person. In truth – how foolish I feel admitting this, but I think it may be fairly common – it never occurred to me that he left me because HE was a bad person. We both behaved badly. His behaviour these days is hurtful and inexplicable but it is not a reflection on me or my children, only on him.

'My ex is no longer connected to me, but she's still behaving in the same self-destructive ways, overspending on her credit card and letting mortgage payments slip. Although it is sad that she is still caught in this loop, it has helped me to see that her behaviour was not my fault – she was bad with money before I came along and she remained so afterwards.' **Len**

It has taken years for me to realise that, in the end, we were a bad couple. I no longer think in terms of a failed marriage: our marriage, like many others, ran its course. We had three wonderful children, and some good times, and ultimately we brought out the worst in one another, which is not that unusual. Some marriages last a long time, and others don't, but I no longer think in terms of failure.

TIP: Talk to yourself as your best friend would.

If you find it hard to talk to yourself as a friend, lacking objectivity in your own circumstances, then listen to what your friends tell you, or join a group like our Making Peace with Divorce group on Facebook, and listen to what the kindly folk there tell you. Don't beat yourself up.

As well as our friendly, supportive Facebook group, you may find it helpful to join a group or attend workshops tailored to your particular circumstances. This will help you to realise that you are not alone, and will allow you to get some objectivity about your situation, which will go a long way towards relieving isolation, confusion and guilt. See p.185 for some examples of these.

'I found the Freedom Programme sessions life-changing, particularly the "effects on children" of remaining in an abusive relationship. We all stay "for the kids" but we underestimate the wider effects of abuse on childen. It's so harmful. Meanwhile, the abuser is playing everything down, and things you've been persuaded are "normal" or accused of "blowing out of proportion" can actually be serious safeguarding issues. Listen to your gut and/or call Women's Aid for an objective perspective of what's going on!' **Maggie**

Yes, there is cause for introspection, for increased self-knowledge (you know my view on the usefulness of therapy) and for the acknowledgement of our own part in our fortunes and misfortunes. But a failed marriage, or a marriage that was a mistake, or that ran its course, should not define you for the rest of your life. It's time to look at making it all official, and ratifying your divorce.

5. 'R' IS FOR REPRESENTATION
RATIFYING A DIVORCE: WHICH ROUTE TO
GO DOWN AND HOW TO CHOOSE A LAWYER

On one level, getting a divorce is simple. It's the dissolution of a marriage or civil partnership contract. You fill in a form and send it to court, get a decree nisi, and six weeks later you can apply for a decree absolute. That's basically it: your marriage or civil partnership is ended. And some people do this. They don't go to court, they don't even use lawyers. That is one end of the scale.

At the other end: the long drawn out and expensive court cases we read about in the papers, with vast sums being spent on legal bills, sometimes even involving prison sentences. Talk about acrimonious!

'Mr Morris now has a six-week prison sentence hanging over his head, which Judge Hughes imposed for non-payment of maintenance but suspended to give him a chance to pay up.' **Daily Telegraph, 14 March 2016**

'A couple fighting over an asset pool of £818,416 incurred such high costs that litigation collapsed and the husband was forced to declare himself bankrupt.' **Guardian, 13 November 2014**

It does not have to be this way. If you can agree between yourselves – amicably or not – you, too, can have a quick and easy divorce. Most experts advise that you should not complete the undoing of the contract (ie get the decree absolute) until agreements are in place regarding money and children. So, it's not the divorce that takes time and money but the wrangling about children and finances. This is what holds up the divorce, eats up money and can also eat up your soul.

For most of us, it's somewhere in between these two extremes in terms of animosity, time and cost. Because, usually, it is not a simple case of undoing a legal contract with a couple of signatures and a court stamp. Emotions are involved. And money.

What follows is a brief outline of the process you might go through and questions you might ask. It is necessarily simplified – there are many more forms and stages than will be tackled here – but we deal with the main and most common aspects and try to give an overview of what can be a complicated process, full of jargon (some of it in Latin) just at a time when you may be feeling particularly overwhelmed. This chapter is for those who are legally married or in a civil partnership.

NOTE: You may be wondering whether you need to get divorced at all. Some couples separate and never feel the need to go through the legal process, others opt for a 'legal separation'[39]. But some don't bother with that either. There may be good reasons for this beyond inertia or religious conviction, such as retaining certain medical or pension benefits and inheritance rights. But do consider whether you are best served by a situation in which you still have a spouse in name and law only.

In this chapter we'll look at the basic hoops you need to go through to legally divorce. I very much hope that in your case, you are able to draw a line under your marriage there. For most people, while painful and protracted, divorce can be achieved without repeated trips to court or enforcement measures. In the UK about

90% of divorces are settled out of court. This chapter is for those 90%. In Chapter 6 we'll focus on next steps; what to do if financial settlement is not achieved so simply and/or there are issues around the children. In both these chapters, please be aware that these pointers do not constitute legal advice.

5.1 Petitioning for divorce

5.1i If you want to begin the divorce

If you've tried counselling and come to the conclusion that the two of you are better apart, what next? Where do you start? Whether you do this with the help of a lawyer or not (see below for more on lawyers), the first step is to *petition*. This, like most of the divorce process, is (mostly) the same whether you are married or in a civil partnership.

> FACT: The form you need is D8 'Divorce/Dissolution/ (Judicial) Separation Petition'.

You can find the form, and notes to help you complete it, online at HM Courts & Tribunals Service[40] or from your local county court. If you're the one filling the form, you are *the Petitioner*. Your ex is *the Respondent*. The form is not hard to complete: it's mostly just stuff like names and dates. The only part that people sometimes struggle with is the 'statement of case', where you put your grounds for divorce.

> FACT: To apply for a divorce or dissolution you have to show that the marriage has 'broken down irretrievably'.

The only ground for divorce is 'irretrievable breakdown of marriage', and there are five categories of proof. Some of the available options are quite straightforward:

- The Respondent has deserted you two years ago or more
- You have lived apart for at least two years and you both agree to the divorce
- You have lived apart for five years (you don't need agreement from your ex)

But two are not. These are:

- Adultery ('and the Petitioner finds it intolerable to live with the Respondent')
- Unreasonable Behaviour

FACT: Citing adultery does not have any effect on any proceedings regarding children or finance. The courts will not take the behaviour of the parties into account unless it is deemed relevant (eg fraud, or unsuitability to be around children), which infidelity is not.

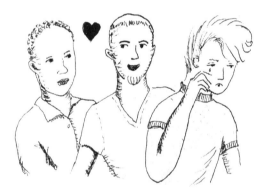

If you are divorcing because your partner has had an affair or left you for another, **you may be tempted to go for adultery. This is not necessarily the best option, no matter how justified you may feel in citing it**. For one thing, if the Respondent does not admit the adultery, it will have to be proven, and the only proof is a child of the union or photographic evidence of actual sexual intercourse (not, for example, kissing or mutual masturbation: the legal definition is very precise). Unlikely. For another, you need to petition within six months of becoming aware of the adultery, otherwise you are deemed to have 'condoned it'. Thirdly, you can use adultery within 'unreasonable behaviour'. And lastly, for the purposes of this form, adultery is not available for same sex couples (though the notes suggest that any adulterous relationship in a civil partnership would also be a same sex relationship, which is clearly not necessarily the case). It used to be that the co-respondent (other man or woman) had to be named but this is no longer necessary.

> FACT: Adultery can only be cited if between the Respondent and a person of the opposite sex.

Therefore, even if infidelity played an important part in the end of your relationship, you may be better served by the fifth ground: unreasonable behaviour.

5.1ii Unreasonable Behaviour

This is the most commonly used. Clearly in some cases, Unreasonable Behaviour could include seriously damaging things like physical or mental cruelty to you or your children. Or being financially irresponsible, or drinking to excess.

In practice, behaviour cited is more commonly illustrative of a lack of communication, lack of sex, lack of shared social life etc. This is also where you can reference an 'improper relationship' if there has been infidelity.

'My husband was very controlling. He would check my Tesco receipts to see what I'd spent on groceries, while buying himself all sorts of expensive things.' **Tracy**

Accepted wisdom is that you need to give a few instances of your spouse's unreasonable behaviour.

TIP: An unwritten rule of thumb: cite the *first*, the *last* and the *worst* instance. I have frequently seen suggestions that you also say in each case how this behaviour made you feel.

The Respondent refuses to sleep in the marital bed, which makes the Petitioner feel unloved.

The Respondent does not take part in any family activities at the weekend, preferring to go out with his friends. The Petitioner is left feeling lonely and abandoned.

The examples can be relatively mild – of the 'lid on the toothpaste' type – because, generally speaking, no judge is going to force a couple to stay married.

TIP: It is a good idea, if relations permit, to show the Respondent what you plan to say (and for this not to be too inflammatory).

'When the petition lands on your doormat, it can be hard. My ex had rung beforehand, and explained that he had written it with the help of his solicitor to achieve our common goal, the least traumatic divorce possible, and he knew it did not represent the full story. He rang again the day after to check I was OK.' **Jean**

You want your spouse not to contest the petition because that will be time consuming, expensive and will wind you both up. So the grounds need to be sufficiently un-antagonistic to get the agreement of the Respondent, while at the same time convincing a judge that they are sufficient to proceed with the divorce.

'I wrote that she called me gay in front of the children and constantly picked fault.' **Tariq**

TIP: Although you do not need to 'big up' the unreasonable behaviour, and you may be fearful of antagonising your ex, if you are genuinely in fear of harm, you may want to mention it in case

you need to rely on having done so later. In cases of domestic abuse, for example, you may be eligible for legal aid.

5.1iii Submitting the form

When you have completed the form, you need to pay a fee (currently £550) and send three copies of the petition to your nearest divorce centre.

TIP: Apparently 40% of forms are rejected, usually for factual inconsistencies around names and dates, so do take care to double check such details.

The court will send the petition to the Respondent by post. Sometimes it is necessary or advisable to send these by hand using a county court bailiff or a process server. If you don't have an address for the Respondent, you need to demonstrate that you have tried to get one.

5.1iv If you are the Respondent

Perhaps it's your partner who has started the ball rolling; maybe you've received the paperwork already or been threatened with it. Whether you want the divorce or not, receiving the form and seeing it all in black and white can be upsetting. Try not to get defensive. Contesting the petition is not a good use of your time or money and will not help the process.

TIP: Remember, other than the two of you and the judge, nobody need ever know what was written[41].

I am struggling to remember now exactly what my own grounds were and I'm fairly confident my ex has no idea. He did not contest them. They were uncontroversial and he wanted the divorce more than I did. I do remember saying that we often argued about money

– later I felt vindicated because afterwards it became clear he had been lying to me about money for years. And I recall that I also gave as one example that he had walked out on us and refused to come back, which surely is undeniably a good reason for divorce? I delayed sending in the forms as I agonised over these few words: they seemed terribly important at the time. I have seen how others have struggled, too. Looking back it all seems less of an issue.

TIP: Whether you agree with what is said or not, it's best to keep your eye on the bigger picture and let it go.

There is another option. You can agree to the divorce but dispute the grounds. But really, though it may seem important to you now, it doesn't change anything, except in cases of danger to life and limb, which we have already mentioned.

If you have received a petition, you must return the acknowledgement of service form D10 enclosed. (If you don't, the Petitioner can proceed as if you have agreed.) You may agree or disagree (ie 'defend' the divorce), whereupon you have 21 days to 'give an answer' and pay a fee. This is not recommended.

5.2 Completing Form E

FACT: Form E is your financial statement.

Divorces (and dissolutions) come in all different shapes and sizes, and there are too many forms to go into here for the various things that could come up. However, many couples are likely to negotiate or have the court order a financial settlement. The starting point in any mediation or lawyer-driven process will be for each party to make what's called 'financial disclosure' by filling in their Form E, so it is a good idea to fill the form even if you are not going the adversarial route.

TIP: Do not lie.

Section 1 – General Information
This first section simply asks for simple facts like names and dates.

Section 2 – Financial Details
Here you will be asked about:

- Your income (from work, investments, benefits)
- Your assets (home, car, jewellery, savings, pension – anything worth more than £500)
- Your liabilities (mortgage, loans, tax owed)
- Your business interests

> If any of these are jointly held (eg a mortgage) your share is presumed to be 50%.

In other words, *how much money do you have*? Since they are trying to capture every kind of income or asset, the form can seem dauntingly long. For people with simpler finances (no trust funds, directorships etc) much of it will not apply. You will need to provide evidence such as payslips, pension valuations, tax assessments etc, so don't leave it too late to get these – if they are not readily available online it can take a while.

TIP: Leave plenty of time to gather information from building societies etc.

'My ex said he given up work. He didn't really, he carried on and took cash-in-hand – so a tip for others in a similar position: look for an absence of cash withdrawals on the bank statements!' **Libbie**

Section 3 - Financial Requirements

You will also be asked *how much money you need*. As our finances had always been left to my banker husband, I was frightened of the section about assets because I wasn't sure I knew what I had. But it was the part about needs that frightened me more. I was terrified of underselling myself and my children if I forgot some expense or other.

At the same time, I was concerned not to be greedy. It was very stressful: I had given up my career to be a stay-at-home mum and was completely without income. At that time I was completely reliant on my ex to provide for us, which he failed to do. We British are famously cagey when it comes to our money, yet kind friends who had been through it shared their own forms, which was a helpful sanity check. And my lawyer suggested things I hadn't thought of, like driving lessons for our teenage children (laughably ambitious, as it turned out, but maybe your case will be different!).

TIP: The boxes are quite small, so do your adding up of details beforehand, eg bus fares and shoes and food, then summarise on the form.

Section 4 – Other Information

This is more narrative, for example 'give brief details of the standard of living enjoyed by you and your spouse/civil partner during the marriage/civil partnership', and here you'd mention things like foreign holidays. 'Any other circumstances' could include that you are disabled, or discrepancies in earning capacity between you and your ex, or the fact that one of you is co-habiting or expects to remarry.

There is also a question about conduct.

> FACT: Bad behaviour or conduct by the other party will only be taken into account in very exceptional circumstances and has to be 'gross and obvious'.

At this point I was just beginning to get glimmers of how my ex had been siphoning funds and secretly going on island holidays and shopping sprees. So I mentioned it (called 'running a conduct case') on my form. I'm not sure whether it made any difference in the end, because I was advised that the court was unlikely to force him into bankruptcy. So though his enormous debts had been run up behind my back and largely post separation, he took a large share of our limited equity when we agreed our settlement.

> FACT: In very rare cases of 'wanton dissipation of assets' these can be 'added back' so that the other party is not disadvantaged, but the resources do need to be there to enable this.

Sadly, it is not unusual for exes to declare themselves bankrupt during or after divorce proceedings. If your ex goes bankrupt within five years of your divorce, there is a chance that you could lose your share. But your ex's creditors would need to demonstrate that funds had been passed to you in order to deprive them of what they were owed. If both of you are legally represented it should be straightforward to show that the two of you were not acting as a team. If you're representing yourself however, situations like this can be much more stressful, so **if alarm bells are ringing about the state of your ex's finances, I'd recommend that you do get some legal support.**

FACT: Subsequent discharge from bankruptcy does NOT release the bankrupt from a debt arising from an order in the family courts.

Section 5 – Order Sought

Here you say what it is you are seeking. For example, whether you are asking for the family home to be sold, whether you are asking for anything in relation to a pension, whether you think this is a case for continuing spousal maintenance. It is fairly straight forward and not binding (partly because you will not have seen your ex's Form E yet).

'One in eight separated women (12%) said they have no pension / savings plans as they were relying on their partner to fund their retirement'. **Aviva report 2014**

A word about spousal maintenance

Especially if you have been financially dependent on your ex during the partnership, you may feel that you should continue to be supported in the future. Perhaps (as in my case) your earning capacity is a fraction of your ex's. You may be frightened that you will not be able to support yourself, as I was after 20 years out of the workforce. All the same, **if funds allow, the courts will prefer a 'clean break',** *and so should you.* **Not only because of the depressingly high proportion of exes (like mine) who defy court orders to pay spousal and child maintenance, but because it will help you to get on with your life if you are not tied to your ex by the expectation or reality of monthly payments.** Depending on your circumstances, this need not mean you have to earn your own keep in the labour market; it may be that you can be awarded a greater share of equity or pension in order to achieve a clean break. I had been so browbeaten that I honestly thought I would rather take income from my banker ex than manage my own affairs. This was a mistake on many levels.

A word about child maintenance

Note the distinction between *spousal maintenance* and *child maintenance*. Usually, the parent with the greater earning power pays child maintenance for any child under 18, and quite often for many years after that, especially if the children are continuing in education. However, sometimes parents agree on some other split, where the higher earner may be relieved of any child maintenance payments in return for a lump sum or a share of the family home.

'I did a deal with my ex – I would keep the house in return for his having to pay no maintenance for the kids, ever. I believe that one of the reasons we now have a civilised, even friendly relationship is because there was a clean break between us with no continuing financial obligations on either side. I realise that this isn't possible for many people and I was fortunate that I was in a position to be able to provide for my kids without any contribution from him.' **Anna**

Statement of Truth

You then sign saying that you have been truthful in the form.

TIP: I repeat, do not lie. If you do, you could find yourself facing additional court proceedings. Plus, it's just wrong.

'There is no pillow so soft as a clear conscience.' **French proverb**

5.3 Do I need a lawyer?

No.

While you do not need a lawyer to legally divorce, there are many reasons you may prefer to use one to a greater or lesser extent. While lawyers are expensive, they can save you money. And in certain cases (eg domestic abuse) you may get legal aid to cover the cost.

'My ex offered only 16% of our joint assets (despite me having sole care of our three young children), but the court would not have allowed that. In the end, I was awarded 42%. My legal advice and support came at a cost, but that was a fraction of what I gained for the children's future. Not to mention my own.' **Maggie**

5.3i Doing without a lawyer

You and your ex partner can agree matters between you, and many couples do this, if things are not too acrimonious or contentious. Even in such a case, it might be as well to employ a lawyer to write up your agreement into a 'consent order' and ask a court to approve it, otherwise it is not legally binding. It is amazing how things that seem perfectly straightforward and unambiguous at the time of writing can turn out to be a can of worms. While relations may seem friendly now, everything can change with the arrival of a new partner, a new child, an inheritance or lottery win. Using a lawyer will at least reduce the chances of expensive legal action following accusations of breach or misinterpretation further down the line, should it come to that.

FACT: If your agreement is not made official, your ex can come back in the future and make a claim on your finances.

Given the high stakes involved, the lack of trust in many cases, the fact that one is likely to be feeling depressed or furious, **many couples quite sensibly decide to have the documents drawn up by a solicitor and made official by the courts.** I have friends who have managed in this way quite successfully, so I know it can be done.

'My ex had visited a solicitor and found out what the whole process was likely to cost if we both employed lawyers. So he agreed to my offer to do most of the work, drawing up a list of assets, and sharing everything. We then just used a solicitor to write it up.' **Ann**

FACT: An agreement that is made between yourselves, and not imposed by a judge, is called a *Consent Order*. In order to have it made official, it is sent to the court and stamped, and it becomes legally binding. An agreement that is ordered by the court is called a *Court Order*.

5.3i.a Representing yourself in court

Even if you and your ex can't agree on things between yourselves, and the matter does go to court, you still don't *need* a lawyer. You can be a 'litigant in person' (LiP) or 'self-repper'. Plenty of people do represent themselves in court, usually because they can't afford to have legal representation.

TIP: Don't think you *can't* represent yourself in court. Many people do, and help is available.

'The judge was very kind. She kept making sure I understood what was going on. I think she realised he was a bully!' **Shona**

Though it can be frightening in many ways, judges and court officials do try to put LiPs at ease, and make sure things are explained to them. Family lawyer Marilyn Stowe has a blog[42] which warns LiPs of some of the pitfalls of self representation, such as not keeping emotions in check, and not knowing where to stop. But don't let that advice put you off. If you can't afford a lawyer, don't qualify for legal aid, and have to go to court, you will need to do it yourself. Many people do so and live to tell the tale! There's a list of tips for self-reppers on Wikivorce[43].

> FACT: Litigants in person are legally entitled to have assistance, lay or professional, unless there are special circumstances.

McKenzie Friends

If mediation fails and you choose, or are forced by your ex, to go to court and are representing yourself, you may want to use a 'McKenzie Friend' (named after a McKenzie v McKenzie case in 1970). This can be an actual friend whose support you value, or a stranger, paid or unpaid, legally qualified or not. They are allowed to accompany you to court and they can also help you with various aspects of your case, though there are things they can't do on your behalf, like file court documents. While a McKenzie Friend is not allowed to speak to the judge, he or she can quietly advise you on what to say. If you are an LiP, and want to find out more, contact McKenzie Friends[44]. They have a 24/7 answer service on 0333 5678 333 or you can email help@mckenzie-friend.org.uk. If you don't already have someone in mind, they can put you in touch with someone to act as your McKenzie Friend.

'I am acting as LiP in my divorce and financial settlement and never in my life have I felt so alone, vulnerable, scared and isolated. I have no money for representation whereas my ex has both solicitors and a barrister. I only found out about McKenzie Friends yesterday but already have a consultation with one next week, and I feel more confident and capable of attending court to pitch myself against the wife's army of paid legals as a result.' **Graham**

5.3ii Nearly doing without a lawyer

5.3ii.a Quickie online divorce

I just typed 'online divorce' into Google. Almost 4 million results in about half a second. Try it. You will see that there are loads of ads offering you a divorce for just £37. The price is misleading because you still have to pay the court fees, which at the time of writing were £550 for the petition and decree absolute (help is available if you are on a low income). All the same, it's obvious that £37 doesn't get you the time of day from most divorce lawyers. So having an online service where (ideally) a solicitor goes over the documents you provide for a very low fixed price is going to save you a load of money. But it will only work if your case is very straightforward and you have a good idea of what is going on. One of my friends used such an online legal offer and was happy with it. But hers was a short, childless marriage, and not her first, so she was an ideal candidate for this kind of no-frills service.

'My divorce was very straightforward. It was a mutual decision and after many years of pain and disappointment was a really positive decision for both of us. I did go to see a solicitor on one occasion to find out my rights on the legal side of things. This one-hour session was free and turned out to be invaluable, but we didn't want to go any further down the personal lawyer route as we didn't want to fork out a fortune. Thereafter we

managed OK going down the online divorce route, and it was very cost-effective, even though we have two children. We started proceedings in April and the divorce was finalised that October. We got sent a number of forms to sign – sometimes it felt like we were waiting an eternity these, but apparently this is standard procedure. The only glitch came when we discussed the finances. It was my ex's expectation that we would divide everything 50/50. However as I already had a house when we got married, it was only fair that I got a larger chunk of the settlement. This initially didn't go down too well, however after thinking about the financial implications of disputing it, he agreed.' **Anita**

5.3ii.b Fixed price divorce

Many family solicitors offer fixed price divorces. This is good but, again, can be misleading. It is not as obvious to the hapless person going through the process as it is to the lawyers but some things are excluded. Things that are likely to rack up hours of a solicitor's time. Mainly concerning the splitting of assets ('financial settlement'). So it's essentially a more tailored service than the online quickie. My own excellent solicitor offered such a package but my final bill was significantly higher because of all the financial shenanigans which involved hours of her time poring over papers from the other side, dealing with forensic accountants (at the insistence of the court) and so on.

TIP: If you are one of the very many separating couples who are renting their home and have little in the way of assets to argue over; if you both earn a similar amount and if you don't have children, a simple fixed price divorce may suit you very well.

5.3ii.c Using a lawyer ad hoc

Remember that **if you represent yourself, you can still pay for legal advice whenever you like on specific issues, as well as for drawing up agreements**. Your lawyer will not be as familiar with your case but, on the other hand, you will not spend much and will be in control of the situation.

'My ex and I used lawyers to help us agree the division of our finances, but thereafter we were able to keep costs down by doing the form filling ourselves. We didn't have to go to court, we just had to make sure the paperwork was submitted at the right time to the right people.' **Sarah**

'I got advice from a solicitor, but in court represented myself so it didn't cost me huge amounts.' **Len**

5.4 How to choose a lawyer

5.4i Choosing a solicitor

After my husband left us and stopped giving us any money, friends said 'GET A LAWYER!' so I did finally start to look around. I still didn't want a divorce, so it was half-hearted. Maybe for that reason I didn't fancy working with any of the ones I met. Just when people were starting to say 'stop looking and just pick one!' I found I could not decide on anything at all. Luckily, a friend sought a recommendation and actually insisted on coming with me, otherwise I might still be waiting for something to happen, afraid to make the first move.

TIP: Personal recommendation is the way to go. Make discrete enquiries: we all know people who have divorced and your friends will normally be happy to talk about their experiences if you ask.

Make an appointment to see a solicitor who comes recommended. There is much talk (online, in books and amongst people who divorced a while back) about solicitors offering a free half hour. That may be so but not in my experience, though some do offer fixed price initial consultations. All the same, a short meeting, at normal rates if necessary, could still save you making an expensive mistake.

TIP: Do not choose someone without meeting. As with builders: if you don't like your solicitor at the beginning, you almost certainly won't by the end.

Note that, especially if you are using an expensive lawyer, you may find that much of the form filling and daily contact with you is done by a junior. Yes, that will be cheaper, but it will not be the lawyer you chose, so meet other team members too if possible. On the other hand, as a lawyer friend of mine points out, his hourly rate may be high, but with his experience he does things better and in half the time of some cheaper lawyers.

If you really don't have any personal recommendations, or if you'd like to research the ones you do have, apart from general Googling, you can always try a directory such as Chambers and Partners[45] which allows you to search for a lawyer according to geographic location and practice area (look for 'family' or 'matrimonial' law; they usually don't use the word 'divorce'). Chambers says they 'identify the best' and rank the firms and individuals in them. Of the half dozen lawyers I met, five worked for firms listed in Chambers, but the one I chose in the end did not. My ex did choose one of the big expensive city firms listed in Chambers, but I would rather have had my lawyer than his at any price.

TIP: Remember: having a cheap lawyer or no lawyer at all may be a false economy.

'It took nearly four years, a huge amount of work, repeated court hearings, plus £35k, to nail down a final settlement. He was used to being able to trample all over me, and I wouldn't have got half the settlement by trying to negotiate with him on my own. It got very nasty, but it's been worth it.' **Laura**

5.4ii Choosing a barrister

FACT: You probably won't need a barrister.

If you need a barrister, again, you may have personal recommendations from friends. But very often the barrister is selected or suggested by your solicitor. This can be a bit hit and miss. And the system does not inspire confidence: you have little contact with your barrister as most will communicate only with the solicitor, so you can't for example, phone or email them directly (though increasingly some are accepting 'direct access'), and yet you rely on them to represent you in court. You may have a good rapport with your solicitor but feel that your barrister is practically a stranger. You can Google these people, but a lot is hinging on them and it felt to me like a high stakes lottery. At my first hearing, I was disappointed by my barrister, and – heart in mouth – I switched to someone else for the next one. It is a risky business. Bear in mind that you don't have to use a barrister; you may want to discuss with your solicitor if one is recommended.

5.4iii Types of lawyers and types of process

Any solicitor can help you if your divorce or separation is a simple one, but most people will choose one experienced and specialised in family law. Beyond this, it is a good idea to go for one who is a member of Resolution[46].

TIP: Look for a lawyer who is a member of Resolution.

Resolution has 6,500 members: family lawyers committed to a non-confrontational approach. People joke about wanting Rottweilers as their divorce lawyers, but those I know who have done this have tended to come away thinking that Rottweilers are not so nice to work with.

My friend: *'I used [lawyer X], who is known for being a complete bitch. And she was!'*

Me: *'To your ex?'*

My friend: *'To me!'*

They don't necessarily get you better results either. Not to mention that you will feel better about yourself if you play nice, even if you sometimes harbour murderous thoughts.

Appointing a lawyer does not mean that you will necessarily go to court. Indeed your lawyer will likely try hard to avoid it. Going to court is expensive; if you end up going all the way to a Final Hearing, it will cost you a fortune if you use a lawyer, and it will be the judge who decides what happens. You therefore run the risk of ending up with a smaller share of a smaller 'pot' of assets.

TIP: Try to avoid going to court, which is expensive, stressful and risky.

If you do end up there, Chapter 6 has some tips on how to make it as painless as possible.

When choosing a divorce lawyer, you may also need to consider the type of process you plan to use because not all lawyers are qualified in each.

5.4iii.a Collaboration

Collaboration is a relatively new way of divorcing, generally agreed to be quicker, cheaper and less painful than the usual, more adversarial approach.

If you and your ex decide to go down this route, each of you will need to appoint a lawyer trained in collaborative law. The four of you commit to working out an agreement without going to court.

Though you can talk to your lawyers privately to prepare, meetings are held 'four way' with both of you and your two lawyers present, and you reach agreements in the meetings. One of the benefits of the collaborative process is that it's not driven by a timetable imposed by the courts. However the main advantage is that, with the four of you talking face to face, it is far less adversarial (and quicker) than the traditional exchange of lawyers' letters. It usually only takes a handful of meetings to reach an agreement, after which the lawyers put the agreement into effect, getting a court order as appropriate. This can work well, but it does require that you and your ex can be in the same room together!

Because of the commitment to avoid court, if the discussions should break down, you will each have to find a new lawyer.

'We decided to look at collaborative divorce because it meant we stood to save more of our meagre assets. At one point Vinnie wanted to give up but we stuck with it because if you decide to abandon collaborative law, you need to start again with new lawyers, which would have sucked up more time and money.' **Milos**

5.4iii.b Mediation

While collaboration involves each of you appointing a collaborative lawyer to represent your interests in a negotiation, mediation usually (not always) involves one mediator who acts as a go-between. He or she will not be on either 'side' but will work to help the two of you to come to an agreement.

Obviously coming to an agreement in this way, if possible, would likely be cheaper, quicker and less adversarial than the traditional route. But it has its drawbacks.

- Mediators are not necessarily legally trained (though you can choose one who is).
- Mediators are there to get to an agreement. Not – necessarily – to ensure that the agreement is fair.

- If one of you is a confident executive used to negotiating and the other a stay at home parent, and distraught, you may not be evenly matched in mediation.
- If one of you has better information (eg has always managed the finances, is not an employee but has their own company so can manipulate his or her affairs) the other is at a disadvantage in any negotiation.
- You are asked to fill in similar forms to those of the court but you are not legally bound to tell the truth and, sadly, many people lie.
- Any agreement reached in mediation has no teeth: it is not legally binding unless drawn up into a Consent Order and stamped by a judge.

Therefore, **while mediation can work well, for success it does rely on a good balance of power, and both parties being honest and relatively well disposed towards one another.**

'For mediation to work you both have to want it to. My ex and I attended; he didn't like a lot of what he was told. However, we did come to an agreement and a Consent Order was drawn up, which he asked to be changed a couple of times. Then when it was all redone as he asked, he refused to sign. A month's wages down the drain, not to mention the emotional cost.' **James**

Family Mediation Information and Assessment Meeting (MIAM)
The Children and Families Act 2014 stipulates that 'before making a relevant family application, a person must attend a Family Mediation Information and Assessment Meeting'.

FACT: You do not have to use mediation between the two of you, but you do need to attend a MIAM.

(There are exceptions, but these are rare and usually involve reported and prosecuted cases of domestic violence or concerns about the welfare of a child.)

This meeting is to assess whether mediation will be suitable in your case or not, but if you don't want to mediate, your reasons will usually satisfy the assessor. You can both attend the meeting, but I went alone, prior to petitioning for divorce, so that I could tick the box saying I had done so. I believe lawyers have two types of mediators they recommend: those for MIAMs and those for actually mediating.

A little aside:
My MIAM was in the home of the mediator, an eccentric woman who looked to be in her seventies. All around were photos of grandchildren, weddings, graduations. I wept for my lost future. Then she told me she was on her third husband. Since then, instead of crying 'why not me?' when I see elderly couples holding hands, I think to myself 'probably newlyweds'.

5.5   Paying for a lawyer

5.5i   How lawyers charge

In most cases lawyers charge for their time. This means you will be charged for every letter they write, including thinking time; for every letter your ex sends that has to be read; for every text back and forth, every call to the court and so on. They tend to bill in increments of minimum six minutes. So **if your lawyer charges, let's say £300 per hour (and many charge more), that's at least £30 every**

time you send a text. Plus VAT, £36. Add telling you every time there's a letter from your ex, drafting replies, discussing with you and incorporating your changes and you can see that it does not take much for there to be a bill for a few thousand pounds each month in which anything happens at all, even without going to court, or paying a barrister, or experts such as forensic accountants or child psychologists.

TIP: Think carefully before you dash off a quick note or make a quick call.

One problem I had was that it wasn't always clear to me what was relevant and what was not (I was out of my depth and stressed) so I included everything I could think of 'just in case' and probably repeated myself as well. Plus, my lawyer is friendly and kind, and I sometimes had to remind myself of the phrase 'your lawyer is not your friend'. (Though actually, I do now consider her a friend!)

5.5ii How much it will cost

We've seen that companies are quoting as little as £37 for a divorce – add court fees that's a minimum of roughly £600 (and I am not sure how often such a low price is achieved in reality). We read in the papers about costs spiralling into the millions. For most of the people I've spoken to, the number was in the thousands or tens of thousands.

Your lawyer should advise you of estimated costs for any action, but it is impossible to predict accurately because so much depends on the behaviour of the other side and possible skeletons in cupboards. (Your own behaviour is likely to be unpredictable as well, of course, as it is all uncharted territory.)

'My divorce cost me about £60k and him about £150k. He took barristers to every meeting, insisted on going to Final Hearing, and lost. The judge made him pay my fees. I'd offered to go through mediation, which would have saved a fortune.' **Katja**

How to minimise costs

- Do as much of the legwork as you can yourself to save using lawyers or even their cheaper assistants.
- Type your basic information (name, address, details of children and assets, dates of birth marriage separation etc) to hand over at the first meeting – this saves time note-taking and therefore cost.
- Agree as much as you can with your ex without involving lawyers, and just present lawyers with the agreement to document (this is not as simple as it might at first appear to the lay person).
- Ask your ex directly, if possible, for things like bank statements to save going via lawyers.
- Find all the information you need about accounts, pensions and other assets (some may take time to arrive) and make a spreadsheet (or write it all down on paper in clear and comprehensive form).
- Get court forms and study them to see what information is required (most come with notes).
- Fill in as much as you can in advance.
- Try not to call or write to your lawyer over every little thing.
- Use the junior or paralegal, who may well be able to answer your question and will be billed at a lower rate.
- For questions like 'when is the hearing scheduled?' ask the secretary who will be cheaper still, or free.
- Make your own copies.
- Make your own phone calls. For example, to the court.
- Do as much research as you can online.
- Get a friend to help you gather paperwork; fill forms etc before handing things to your lawyer.
- Remember, your lawyer is not your therapist or your friend, so try not to spend hours venting on the phone or in letters.
- Remember, you can always represent yourself and spend money on a lawyer for advice on individual issues.

TIP: Remember as well, that if you are going to use a lawyer, you should put a certain amount of faith in his or her expertise!

5.5iii Affording legal help

While you do not *need* a lawyer, be aware that not using one could end up costing you dear. Only you can decide, but if you feel you need legal representation and haven't the money, can't borrow from your bank or family and friends, there are other options.

Matrimonial loans

'I can't afford a lawyer until I get my settlement!' Catch-22: many people going through divorce or dissolution of civil partnership may be cash poor but asset rich: their main asset – their home – is likely to be sold in the wake of the separation but until then there is no cash for the lawyer. That's where matrimonial loans come in. You can agree a loan that will take you right up to a final hearing; interest is charged only on what you actually draw down as you go along to pay your lawyer. Please note, however, that this should only be considered as a last resort: the interest charged is high, and repayment is due at the end of the case. If you are relying on the sale of your home, for example, to pay it back, you could run into difficulties.

Free help

FACT: Legal aid is no longer available for divorce (except in rare cases, see below).

Legal aid is now only available in cases of domestic abuse or if social services are trying to remove a child from your care. To qualify, you need to be on a low income and not have significant assets. For more information about legal aid in family law cases see the charity Rights of Women[47] and their PDF[48].

While you can no longer expect legal aid in most cases, there is free help available.

- Some (few) lawyers offer a free half hour or so. (Check before going as otherwise you may receive a bill.)
- Bar Pro Bono[49] is a charity which helps to find free legal assistance from volunteer barristers.
- Citizens Advice Bureaus[50] (CAB) are there to 'provide the advice people need for the problems they face'. You can access their advice online, via phone or face to face in their offices. In my experience they are more geared up to dealing with debt, benefit and housing issues, but they may be able to refer you to solicitors who offer free or fixed price initial interviews.
- Law centres[51] give free legal advice and you can find your local office from the Law Centres Network. Not all of them deal with family law but some do.
- You may have heard that some insurance policies cover legal expenses and that organisations, such as Trade Unions, banks or motoring organisations or Which may offer free or cheap legal advice to members or subscribers. True, but matrimonial law is usually excluded.
- There are many sources of legal help online, many of which also have telephone helplines as well as guides and forums.
  - Gingerbread
  - Sorting out Separation[52] (part of a government initiative)
  - Coram Children's Legal Centre[53]
  - Gov.uk
  - Rights of Women
  - Wikivorce
- Many law firms also provide online guides.

- Relate[54] has lots of useful information on its site.
- Don't forget good old-fashioned books but remember that these can quickly become out of date unless they're regularly revised, like this one!

The vast majority of divorces settle without going to court, and very few indeed make it to final hearing. I hope yours will be one of the many. I'd hoped mine would be, too, and honestly believed it would. There we were, two well-intentioned and intelligent people who loved our children and wanted to behave amicably. We avoided a final hearing, but, sad to say, we did go to court. Chapter 6 is for those of you who also find yourselves there.

6. 'C' IS FOR CONFLICT
WHAT IF THINGS DON'T GO SMOOTHLY?

In an ideal world, if people fell out of love, they would simply go their separate ways, wishing one another well, and continuing to keep the best interests of their children at the forefront of their minds. They would be fair and reasonable and accept the situation. We all know this is rarely the case. Even where we try hard, we often fail.

People who behave badly usually do so because they are hurt or fearful, and separation can trigger hurt and fear in spades. If you have been together a while, you're likely to have shared assets, whether you are married or not, and what was lovingly shared is now often bitterly fought over. And for many, unfortunately, children can also become a battleground. Sparks will fly and tears will be shed. Frankly, our adversarial legal system, with the best will in the world, can sometimes make things worse.

For those who have experienced an escalation of hostilities, in this chapter we help you to prepare for court if all attempts to avoid it have failed. Remember: we are still trying to Make Peace with Divorce, and to make things better, not worse!

Below we talk about:

- Going to court over money
- Going to court over children
- Enforcing court orders

NB We do not deal here with the fortunately rarer extreme cases involving domestic violence, child abuse or abduction. These are very serious and should be taken seriously – seek help from organisations such as those below. Obviously, if you or your children are in immediate danger at any time you should call 999.

- Women's Aid – womensaid.org.uk
- Refuge – refuge.org.uk
- Women's Aid / Refuge
  nationaldomesticviolencehelpline.org.uk
  NB also has 24 hour confidential helpline 0808 2000 247
- Men's Advice Line 0808 801 0327 – mensadviceline.org.uk
- Gallop (for LBGTQ people) 0800 999 5428 – gallop.org.uk

In some cases, you or your ex will, for example, not be able to have unsupervised contact with your children, and this will all be dealt with through the courts with the help of social workers.

6.1 Going to court

6.1i What to expect

Most of us have not set foot inside a courtroom before and it can be very daunting. My ex had been to court many times but I never had and I was scared of the whole thing, and of him. I had no real idea what would happen, that we would have to walk to the courtroom together, that I would not know where to sit and so on. It was not like on TV. My lawyer and barrister sat in the front, I sat alone behind them. On the other side of the room my ex sat beside one of his lawyers and behind the rest. We were not invited to speak (though my ex did interject). The judge, who presumably had had a half hour or so to peruse the 'bundles' presented by both sides, would shuffle papers and ask questions of the barristers, stopping occasionally to stare piercingly at the Petitioner and Respondent. It's odd: people talk about you as if you are not there, using phrases like 'The wife has done such and such' and 'In the husband's Form E he says...'

TIP: Get to court early. There is very little room, and you want to stake out a private space for yourself and your support team, not find yourself huddled in the same corridor as your ex and his or her legal entourage.

There is a lot of waiting around, you will likely be tired and emotional and will want privacy, not least because you may well find yourself deciding on negotiating strategies between meetings with the judge.

TIP: Be on your guard if chatting in the loos – one of my ex's team emerged from a cubicle!

TIP: Be prepared: you could well be there all day.

Make sure someone can pick up your children from school if necessary: you don't know how long you will be. Bring things like water to drink, layers of clothing to add or shed depending on the temperature, coins for vending machines, a charger for your phone. Tissues. A notebook or pad and something to write with: you might want to make notes for yourself, or pass a note to your lawyer. I also brought a photo of my children to remind me why I was there, not that I could forget. Knitting, or a book to read if you think that might help during down time. And if you're feeling wobbly, let us know in Making Peace with Divorce on Facebook and then members may well pick up your post and cheer you on.

6.2 Fighting over money

Negotiations to and fro are one thing and perhaps only to be expected. But if you can't reach a settlement, you go to court.

TIP: Avoid going to court if you can. You will almost certainly end up spending more than you could possibly gain and will drive yourself crazy.

Everybody is told this but few take it to heart. Positions get entrenched, perhaps to the point where it seems inconceivable to you that the judge will not see the justice of your own position. After months (or years!) of legal wrangling, with stressful preparation for stressful hearings, you can easily spend a fortune if you use lawyers much, and possibly gain little but grey hair and bitterness. I never thought this would happen with me and my ex but in the end we did spend a shameful amount of money that could have been put to better use.

> 'The husband and wife spent what the judge described as "an eye-watering total" of £920,000 from their total joint assets of almost £3m on lawyers and experts. In eight months, said Mr Justice Mostyn, the couple [...] spent almost a third of everything they had built up together over nearly 18 years.' **Guardian 13 November 2014**

TIP: Sometimes the only ones who win are the lawyers.

> 'Divorce is a game played by lawyers.' **Cary Grant**

If one or other of you won't settle, you need to make an application to court. In the UK when a financial application is made to the divorce courts, there are three court hearings scheduled, the first usually about three months away. This does not mean you will necessarily have to attend all or any of these, because agreement can still be reached up to and including the day of a hearing. Try to build bridges if you possibly can.

6.2i First Directions Appointment

This hearing, the first meeting with a judge, is generally short. Petitioner and Respondent are not normally called upon to speak, no evidence is examined and the court won't make an order. However, at this meeting you do need to provide information to enable the judge to 'make directions' towards resolving the dispute.

TIP: Templates for these are available online[55].

Form E
We read in the previous chapter about the Form E, in which each of you makes financial disclosure. By the First Appointment, these forms should have been exchanged and are submitted.

Statement of issues
This is a list of issues in dispute, such as housing needs, earning capacity, how the proceeds of the home should be divided, whether there should be periodical payments (maintenance) or a pension sharing order.

Chronology

In addition, each party will have prepared a Chronology. This is a brief history of the facts that each deems relevant and is done to provide the judge with some context. You need to provide key dates such as:

- The date of your cohabitation
- The date of your marriage
- When you purchased the family home
- The date of any significant inheritance, with amount
- The dates of birth of any children
- Date of separation
- Date of petition
- Date Form Es were exchanged plus, for example, 'delay was on the Wife's side'

Questionnaire

You will have had an opportunity to examine your ex's Form E (assuming it has been submitted on time). If you are perfectly satisfied with the information your ex has provided you need not make a Questionnaire. Otherwise, this is where you can list any information which you believe is missing or misleading. You can include requests for:

- Proof of income
- Valuations of assets
- The nature of cohabitation
- Undeclared capital

Eg 'Re Paragraph[56] 2.3 of Form E: The Petitioner's main account is Barclays 1234567. However, there appear to be very few cash withdrawals from this account. Can the Petitioner please explain this anomaly and whether there is another account from which cash is withdrawn? If so, please can she provide 12 months' bank statements for that account?' The judge decides whether the questions need to be answered. NB If the response to your Questionnaire is unsatisfactory, you can make a Schedule of Deficiencies.

TIP: In many cases, though it may stick in your craw, it will be cheaper to ignore missing information than to pursue it through the courts.

Form G

This indicates whether it would be possible for the First Appointment to proceed as a Financial Dispute Resolution hearing (FDR), which would otherwise be scheduled for a future date. A reason you might not be ready could be that you have not yet received the other party's Form E or other necessary information.

6.1ii Financial Dispute Resolution Hearing

If no agreement has been reached at the initial hearing or since, the case proceeds to FDR. By now both parties should have all the information they requested. You should both come with a proposal for settlement. The judge may give an indication of what he or she thinks of these, may suggest an alternative solution, and could say what he or she might order if the case were to go to trial.

TIP: Though judges do not all agree, you would be wise to take heed of the judge's view rather than cling to the belief that this one is no good and the next one will side with you.

It is in everyone's interest to prevent the case going to trial, so after coming before the judge at the FDR the two parties (with lawyers, if any) are invited to sharpen their pencils, see if they can agree, and come back later to present the outcome of further negotiation to a judge.

TIP: If you haven't agreed yet, do so now to avoid further cost and stress.

'At FDR we were probably not that far apart, yet we could not agree. Predictably, continuing the fight cost us a lot of money, never mind stress. My own case seemed so obviously modest and reasonable that I could not believe that my ex, an investment banker, would continue to claim penury.' **Eliza**

'I am firm. You are obstinate. My ex is a pig-headed fool.' **Bertrand Russell (paraphrased)**

It is not possible for the court to impose an agreement at the FDR. However, if you have broad agreement at this stage, it can be written up in summary ('Heads of Agreement') to be worked up by the Applicant's lawyer into a Court Order and presented to the court for approval and made official.

'In the heat of the moment, [the divorcing couple] can forget that a good settlement is one where both parties walk away thinking that each of them could have done better. That is the price they pay for achieving resolution. I think it is a small price'. **Marilyn Stowe, family lawyer**

If no agreement has been reached, the judge will set a date for a Final Hearing. In addition, the judge will specify if further information is required such as reports by experts. There will be a few months in which to gather whatever is necessary and during this time you would still be well advised to settle.

TIP: It's still not too late to avoid a Final Hearing!

6.2iii Final Hearing

> FACT: At a Final Hearing the decision is taken out of your hands. The judge orders what each of you will receive and what you will have to do.

In my case we failed to agree even at FDR. The judge ordered various things, like the appointment of forensic accountants to look into my ex's businesses, and scheduled us for a four day Final Hearing some months later.

> FACT: A Final Hearing is a trial. You will be cross-examined. Witnesses may be called.

This does not sound like most people's idea of a good time. On top of which, it is very expensive. My barrister asked me for £20,000 to prepare for it. That would have been just the start. There are solicitors to pay for as well, and even if you are representing yourself and so have no lawyer's bills, there is the time off work, the effort of preparation and the risk that things may not go your way. It is stressful and best avoided if possible. I hadn't the money or the stomach for the fight, and tried again to resolve things between us. We'd had lots of meetings in cafes in the early days, during the course of which I felt he reneged on every agreement (he claims it was me but I have the recordings!). This time we agreed to meet with lawyers present. In the end, the process, though it went on beyond the date of the scheduled hearing, resulted in an agreement and so in my case, a Final Hearing was avoided.

If you do go to a Final Hearing, you will come before a different judge than at the FDR, who will not be aware of any 'without prejudice' offers made previously.

'Whatever has happened before, think of the Final Hearing as a clean slate. The new judge won't know what was said before and will try to reach agreement. This really is your last chance.' **Harry**

Before the hearing, both parties and the judge are provided with a Bundle, which is a file of relevant documents. The Applicant (ie the person applying to the court) is usually responsible for preparing the Bundle – if represented his/her lawyer will do it. It needs to be done in accordance with Practice Direction 27A, which describes rules concerning what goes in, how documents are presented and what gets shared with the other side and when – for more information see justice.gov.uk[57].

TIP: Even if neither of you is ordered to produce a Bundle, it is a good idea to come to court with relevant papers, and for this information to be identical in three copies so that you can all refer to them efficiently.

Each side should also come to court armed with a *Position Statement* as part of the Bundle. Here you outline the situation and say what you want the court to do to resolve the dispute. You might say what percentage of which asset should go to whom, whether maintenance should be paid, what is to happen to any pensions and so on. The statement should conform to Practice Direction 22A[58].

TIP: Judges don't always read statements: keep it short.

The lawyer (if there is one) for the applicant will make an opening speech, then both you and your ex (and any witnesses) will give evidence and be cross-examined. Each lawyer makes a closing speech. Like on TV.

TIP: The judge should be addressed as Sir or Madam.

'If we had gone to trial, I understand I could have asked to be excused from cross-examination, on account of my autism. (I like to think I would have taken the stand – I was 100% prepared, having done most of the donkey work myself, and I had absolutely nothing to hide – but

it was reassuring to know I could have ducked out if necessary.) That knowledge helped to keep the stress levels down in anticipation.' **Libbie**

If the case is a simple one, the judge will briefly retire to consider the judgement. If more complex, you will have to come back another day to hear it. The judgement will include whatever orders the judge considers appropriate and that is that. Though there are people who emerge victorious from a final hearing, the most likely outcome is that you will both feel aggrieved, very tired, and poorer.

'I would urge anyone to try and settle out of court. From my experience with a final hearing, I felt the whole process was pointless, a waste of money and a waste of endless tears and stress.' **Layla**

6.1iv Maintenance Pending Suit

If one of you relies on the other for money, and that is not forthcoming during the period in which you are involved in settling your finances as part of your divorce, the financially dependent partner can apply to the courts for interim payments or *Maintenance Pending Suit (MPS)*. This is a temporary arrangement to allow the financially weaker partner to get by and can be arranged quite quickly.

TIP: If at all possible, arrange something without applying to court: it will be cheaper.

Before you apply, you need to have tried to get the money directly. If this fails, use Form A, the same form for applying for financial relief, which can be downloaded from HM Courts & Tribunals Service[59].

A court date is set, and the two of you need to file a sworn statement of income and outgoings. The basis for deciding on MPS is 'reasonableness' and takes into account standard of living prior to separation. The court looks at the income of the applicant for MPS and decides if there is a need. If there are housing costs, especially with children, then the needs of the applicant take priority over other outgoings of the payer. I was a student when I was left with an enormous mortgage and three children in private school, and my ex had stopped paying us anything at all. However, my lawyer and I took the view that since my ex was presenting his affairs in a way that was opaque but seemed to indicate that he had no money, we would just get on with the divorce settlement and save time and money on filing for MPS. We did not expect that the process would take as long as it did in the end. I took in lodgers and sold jewellery and furniture (by this time it was clear I would be moving to a much smaller property despite his original promises!) and tried to stave off eviction by the mortgage company. Had he been an employee, I would have stood a better chance of getting MPS. It is not uncommon, unfortunately, for people who are self employed or own businesses, to manipulate things to their advantage.

'Luckily I had proof that my hubby spent £800 a month gambling, so he could afford to give his children and me a helping hand.' **Suki**

'In March last year, Mrs Justice Parker, sitting at the High Court [...] approved £5,500 a month interim payments while the final divorce settlement was decided. [...] Mrs Villiers [...] has asked for maintenance payments to be increased to £10,000 a month.' **Evening Standard 6 July 2017**

6.3 Fighting over children

When separating couples turn to the courts it is often because of money but sometimes it is to do with the children.

The main bone of contention as regards children (apart from the financial aspects) is contact with or access to them. Sadly, when relations between parents are bad, the children can get caught up in it. They can struggle with not wanting to take sides, not wanting to hurt their parents, or, conversely, wanting to punish them. Even if neither parent sets out to do so, both are often accused by the other of 'poisoning the children' or 'using them as weapons', which undoubtedly does happen sometimes. The situation can become very fraught. As a result, sometimes the non-resident parent (often, but not always, the father) feels that he or she does not see enough of the children. Many are understandably vociferous in campaigning for the rights of fathers. Equally, many resident parents (often, but not always, the mother) feel that the non-resident parent is not sufficiently available for their children. Indeed, sometimes non-resident parents find the situation too painful and absent themselves altogether. Obviously this is to be avoided if you possibly can. At the other extreme, some take matters into their own hands and in rare cases even abduct their children, sometimes taking them to foreign jurisdictions. In some (also thankfully rare) cases, one parent feels that the other poses a risk to their children.

So, for any number of reasons, cases can come to court.

FACT: Remember it is not the rights of the mother or father but the rights of the *child* that are paramount in the eyes of the court. Indeed, even if the parents come to an agreement, the court/CMS still has jurisdiction to make orders, as the right on behalf of the children remains.

'Sometimes it's OK to seek to limit or structure access or let the children make up their own minds (if age appropriate) about whether they want to see the absent (if abusive) parent. Access cannot be denied by either parent, but if the court orders no, or limited, access, it's because the children are at risk of physical or psychological harm from the absent parent.' **Maggie**

'It is well recognised that negotiated agreements between adults generally enhance long-term co-operation, and are better for the child concerned. Therefore, separated parents and families are strongly encouraged to attempt to resolve their disputes concerning the child outside of the court system. This may also be quicker and cheaper.'
justice.gov.uk

Child Arrangements

The Justice website has a useful guide[60], lots of information, and lists of resources for dealing with child arrangements. Another good source of clear guidance is gov.uk[61].

CAFCASS (Children and Family Court Advisory and Support Service) represents children in family court cases, and is independent of the courts, social services, education and health authorities and all similar agencies. Their website[62] has information about what might happen in the family court and how to avoid it.

The process is similar to that described above for financial proceedings: after you apply for an order, the court will arrange a 'directions hearing' at which a judge or magistrate will try to understand what you can or can't agree, and whether your child or children are at risk in any way. There will usually be a family court advisor from CAFCASS at the hearing, and they will usually have sent you information and contacted you beforehand. At court, you will be encouraged to reach an agreement there and then (in which case a consent order can be drawn up). If there is no agreement, the court may ask you to go to a mediator.

'I would suggest that initially you try mediation. Only if that fails should you think about issuing court proceedings as they always increase animosity in the short term, take up to a year to settle and cost thousands.' **Charlie**

If you and the other parent cannot agree between yourselves on arrangements for your children, the court will decide.

> FACT: A judge or magistrate will only make an order if they think it's in the child's best interests.

There are various types of order that it is in the court's power to make. Anyone with parental responsibility can apply for one. Others, like grandparents, can apply but need permission from the courts first.

Parental Responsibility, what is it and who has it?
Parental responsibility is defined in the Children's Act 1989 (CA 89) as all the rights, duties, powers, responsibilities and authorities which by law a parent of a child has in relation to the child and the child's property. In practice this means if you have PR you can make or be involved in decisions such as where a child should live, where a child should go to school, changing a child's name, medical treatment such as whether a child should be inoculated etc.

The biological (birth) mother of a child automatically has Parental Responsibility (PR). For the father, or other parent in same sex relationships, the rules about PR are complicated and depend on whether you were married as well as (because of changed rules) on when the child was born. On adoption, PR is transferred to the adopter(s) and the adopted child loses all legal ties with his or her original parents. Unmarried fathers and other people can acquire PR by various means including court orders.

Gingerbread has a factsheet available on the subject[63].

6.3i Child Arrangements Orders

These orders specify:

- Where your child lives
- When your child spends time with each parent
- When and what other contact (eg phone calls) should occur

'Child Arrangements Orders' replace 'Residence Orders' and 'Contact Orders'.

Child Arrangement Orders (CAOs) apply to both parents. If either of you violates the terms of the order (for example returning a child late after contact) you risk being taken back to court with an application for, for example, a reduced level of contact. To apply for a CAO you need Form C100 (available from HMCTS[64]) and you need to have attempted mediation or attended a MIAM (see Chapter 5 above), except in cases of domestic abuse. CAOs tend to be quite detailed and written in very clear terms so that everyone understands how to comply and is aware if they are in breach.

'My partner has been through court to get contact agreed and it is a living nightmare, so don't go there if you can help it.' **Pat**

6.3ii Specific Issue Orders

These are used to address specific issues such as where the children should go to school and whether they should be brought up in a particular religion.

6.3iii Prohibited Steps Order

A Prohibited Steps Order restricts a parent's ability to exercise their parental responsibility rights.

6.3iv Child Arrangements Programme

The CAP applies where a dispute arises between separated parents or families about arrangements concerning children. It is designed to help reach safe and child-focused agreements, ideally out of court, and is the procedure the courts must follow in family cases, if a court application is made, to encourage swift resolution. A simple flowchart showing the procedure is available at familycourtinfo.org.uk[65].

6.3v Child Contact Interventions

CCIs are short term interventions when it is assessed that a child should be spending time with a parent/adult, but they are not doing so for whatever reason. A CCI is used to assist in establishing safe and beneficial contact for adult and child and to enable the parents/adults in the child's life to work together at maintaining and developing contact independently in the future. This programme is funded by CAFCASS and there is more information on the CAFCASS website[66].

6.4 Enforcing a Court Order

So you've either agreed a Consent Order, or been through the gruelling and costly experience of going to court to get a Court Order (or you have been dragged there by your ex). Ideally, this will be the end of it: both of you now know where you stand and get on with your lives, complying with whatever has been ordered by the court.

Would that it were always so. Sadly, these orders are sometimes ignored. Sometimes people don't do what they have been ordered by the court to do. Some people follow the maxim: Possession is Nine Tenths of the Law. If your ex is keeping your child from you, or refusing to co-operate with the sale of the home (he or she lives there and you don't), or simply not coughing up money that the court has ordered they pay, then what?

If your ex is not following the order, you can ask the court to enforce it. This can have serious repercussions.

6.4i Enforcing child arrangements

For enforcing Child Arrangements Orders, complete form C79 available to download[67] (with guidance CB5[68]), and send it to the court nearest to you that deals with cases involving children (which you can find via the UK government's Court Tribunal Finder service[69]). This will cost £215.

> *'Enforcement hearing adjourned to be heard alongside next contact hearing. Cost so far: £6000. Cost to ex: nil. Emotional cost: immeasurable.'* **Peter**

A 2015 blog post[70] by John Bloch on the Stowe family law firm website, describes a reported case H-R Children. Repeated orders were made over many months for the father in the case to have contact with his two children. Each time the mother failed to comply with the order, and failed to attend court. Eventually the father, in desperation made an application for the mother's committal to prison. A 21 day suspended committal order was made, and after further failures by the mother to comply, the mother was indeed ordered to be sent to prison.

6.4ii Enforcing financial arrangements

For enforcement of a financial order, complete form D50K[71], 'Notice of Application for Enforcement by such method of enforcement as the court may consider appropriate'. The court has fairly wide ranging powers to enforce its orders, up to and including a penal sentence. It can make the following orders:

- Attachment of Earnings Order – funds taken from wages
- Third Party Debt Order – funds taken from a third party such as a bank
- Charging or Stop Order – funds taken from the value of your property

The court can order a Writ or Warrant of Execution (ie seize and sell personal property) and can appoint a receiver. Any of these can be extremely stressful for all concerned, not only to the Respondent, so should only be sought as a last resort.

Remember: you both signed your consent or court order right next to the words 'I understand the undertaking that I have given, and that if I break my promise to the court to pay any sum of money, I may be sent to prison'.

In the case of Pocock v Pocock, Her Honour Judge Moir, finding that the ex husband had repeatedly not complied with orders to pay the mortgage on the home of his former wife, said: "...*this cannot go on. It cannot go on, on the basis that there are continuing returns to court; it cannot go on, on the basis that the stress which is occasioned every month to [the wife] and resulting in court appearances. The Order was made, it was a Consent Order, there was legal representation and the Order must be complied with.*" She therefore made a 14-day order of imprisonment against the husband, suspended as long as he paid the mortgage but to be activated if there were any further breach.

'I feel it's important for men to recognise their responsibility and contribute to the upkeep of their children so I always tried to give the mother of my son a realistic amount each month. However, I don't earn

a lot, and after we split up, found myself getting into deeper and deeper debt. Things came to a head when an accident forced me to stop working for a couple of months. Not for the first time, my ex threatened to stop my son seeing me if I didn't pay. Because I'm self-employed, I only had statutory sick pay to live off so I had nothing to give her. In the end I took myself and my son to live with my parents while I recuperated and I gave my ex my sick pay, while my parents kept us warm and fed. But the time not working gave me pause for breath, and I realised we couldn't continue as we were. My ex and I were never married but I wanted to put a stop to the emotional blackmail and have a proper financial settlement agreed, in writing, so I took her to court. Upon seeing what I'd been paying hitherto, the judge told my ex that she was already getting more than the CSA would calculate I should pay and advised her not to pursue it further, so she didn't.' **Len**

6.4 Next steps – all about the future

I think we've made clear our advice to avoid court if at all possible, but even two well-meaning people can sometimes find themselves locked in a battle that they cannot resolve themselves. Things can turn nasty, and sometimes years down the line. Just when you think you are over the worst of it, some issue or other might rear its head. Nonetheless, I hope the overview we've provided in the six chapters so far help you negotiate the tricky terrain, and where the information has proven insufficient, you've found the signposts to further sources helpful.

Now it's time to turn our attention away from your ex partnership and look to the future, and your new, emerging self.

7. 'E' IS FOR EMERGENCE
HOW TO MAKE A GREAT FUTURE FOR YOURSELF AFTER SEPARATION

The period after separation has its ups and downs – not for nothing is it often referred to with that old cliché: rollercoaster. Sometimes you may feel exhilarated, yet significant dates, memories of old times, consciousness of what you have lost, snatches of songs or a fleeting expression on the face of your child can bring on tears or anger.

'Today would have been our 30ᵗʰ anniversary and although I no longer wish we were still together, I can't stop crying.' **Miriam**

'My ex was an electrician and pretty handy, so every time I have to get a man in to do a simple job around the house I feel annoyed and have to remind myself of all the things I don't miss!' **Bhavya**

'I thought I would be over the moon when I received my decree absolute, but now it is finally all over, I just feel flat.' **Eddie**

143

'I'm OK – sometimes I am truly happy – but when something goes wrong health-wise, desolation can still wrap its dark blanket over me.' **Ann**

Try not to listen to those (including your own inner voice) who say you should be 'over it' by now; should have 'moved on'. 'These are your feelings, so honour them,' says Sarah. 'Fighting emotions, and telling yourself you "should" be different, often prolongs rather than reduces suffering. Making peace with any difficult experience such as divorce, involves acceptance and self-compassion, rather than self-flagellation.'

Over time, and especially if you take the trouble to reflect and grow, the highs and lows become less violent and further apart, and you become increasingly able to look back dispassionately or even fondly on your old self and the person you were in love with, as Sarah has found. 'After our divorce, my ex and I weren't on speaking terms for several years. This was his choice, not mine, but I respected it as he needed time to heal. Then, three years ago, something shifted. He sent me a short email saying he'd noticed there had been bad car crash close to where I live, and he knew it was unlikely I'd been caught up in it but still, he wanted to check I was OK. I sensed a door opening, so tentatively, I pushed: I replied that I was fine, but I was touched he should ask, and said I would really love to hear his news, and shared some of mine. Since then our communications have been genuinely affectionate. Not romantic – we have both had relationships since and have no desire to rekindle anything – but caring. We still don't 'speak' as such – he lives hundreds of miles away – but we email from time to time, and there's a shorthand that we have, as we know one another very well.'

As you begin to reconcile with your circumstances you will, I hope, find increasing joy in your new life. Read on for some tips about getting there!

But first, a few words from others who have emerged after a bruising separation, and who have, each in their own way, made peace with divorce. Over to you…

7.1 Stories from others who've been there

7.1i Maggie, who's no longer trapped and scared

After an 18-year abusive relationship, I desperately wanted out. I would tell friends, "If only I could snap my fingers and be six months the other side of divorce, I would do it right now." But I stayed. I'd convinced myself if was better for the children (it wasn't), but mostly, I was too scared to deal with the fallout from trying to leave again (I'd already tried several times) and staying was definitely the lesser of two evils. I felt completely trapped.

One day a friend took me for a long walk and said, "You *do* have a choice, you know? You *choose* to stay because leaving is harder. But that doesn't mean you *can't* leave." It seems so obvious now, but I hadn't seen I had a choice. *I was that disempowered.* It probably took me another year but, eventually, – after a particularly intense period of gaslighting – I became suicidal (again), and I knew I had to get out. In the end the choice was simple – I couldn't bear the thought of killing myself and leaving the kids in his sole care.

That was nearly five years ago. I've had to fight every inch of the way (I've lost count of the number of court hearings), and although the fight has rendered me completely dysfunctional with anxiety at times, it has – in the long term – made me immeasurably stronger. My divorce finally came through last year, and as soon as the family house is sold, it will all be over. It won't ever be over, of course; but the most important lesson I've learned is that *the biggest hold anyone has over you...is your fear of what they think.*

He can think what he likes, say what he likes, do what he likes, tell anyone whatever he likes, and none of it changes who I am... *the person I know myself to be.* And I'm a hundred times stronger than the person I used to be.

7.1ii Helen, who is rediscovering childhood pleasures

One of the most important things for me on moving forward was the establishing of new traditions. Where I would think 'Oh, we always used to....', I set a new tradition. This was a lovely thing to do and a real step forward, the establishing of a new history. The second thing was to recall things that I used to love doing when I was younger and re-find those. Such as juggling... writing... Saturday-put-the-world-to-right-coffees with friends. We all have things we used to do earlier in our lives, before the relationship that made us happy. In addition, there is the doing of new things we always wanted to do or find we want to do. All of these things were me moving forward and beyond the heartbreak into a new life.

7.1iii Ann, the survivor with a special group of friends

It is seven years to the day that my ex called a halt to our marriage in the basest way. His cruelty, greed and spite never abated and I have not spoken to him or heard from him for four years – we were married for nearly 30. Since that day, in spite of being thrown into a suicidal abyss, I am transformed. Initially with the help of a wonderful doctor who did everything right – I am now much healthier – and then with the surprising support of a circle of very special friends, old and new. I have been able to explore my interests and been introduced to new ones. I am not wealthy, and I thought that would be a problem, instead I have discovered that you

don't need much to live well. Just to survive I had to learn to be kind to myself and like the woman I am, rather than always look at my shortcomings. Today friends tell me that I exude a calm, happy aura – I love that.

7.1iv Debi, now remarried happily after much heartbreak

My first marriage broke up because we had problems conceiving. We didn't get pregnant and eventually our relationship broke under the strain. My heart was broken, I thought I'd never be happy again. When my job as a nursing assistant came to an end after the third hospital I worked in was closing, I decided a change was needed: I started working in a factory. On the first day I saw Colin, and just *knew* I would marry him! Over two decades later, we have been wed for 13 years with an almost 11-year-old adopted son and I couldn't be happier! So to anyone caught up in the midst of it, I'd like to say that there is a new future out there, waiting. It may not be what you think, and it may not arrive exactly when you wish, and it may not involve another relationship, but you can be happy, and what doesn't break you makes you stronger.

7.1v Julio, who is enjoying the single life

I've been separated five years now, and it's about three years since our bruising divorce. I'm in my early fifties, and at first when I found myself alone, I felt old and more or less thought my life was over. Surprisingly, as I've picked myself up and shaken off the past, I've found I'm having a lot of fun.

My kids are grown up and I have a good relationship with them. They tell me their mum is out clubbing. They are embarrassed that she is dating guys about their age. I don't really care what she does – good luck to her.

Friends have set me up on a few dates. My female friends have been particularly keen to pair me up. But whilst my mates are great, some of their single friends have seemed a bit bonkers, or lonely and desperate, which I find off-putting, though maybe they'd say the same about me. Sod's law, the one I found most attractive was still in love with her ex – they'd only split up a couple of months before we were introduced and I decided I was better off single.

So now I'm exploring some of the ambitions I had when I was younger – I've been learning to paraglide – which I really enjoy, and I'm thinking of forming a band with some mates, so maybe I embarrass my kids as much as their mum! Though I'm not trying to relive my youth, just have a laugh. Of course things are different in middle age, and I can't go back to the way I was at 21. But there are advantages to that. Life is good.

7.1vi Anna, who now gets on with her ex

My husband left me for another woman and our relationship was very bad in the beginning. It improved enormously when I started dating again and realised that I was happier without him. It improved exponentially when the floozie he left me for, left him! So much so, that I had to make it clear to my sons that we would not be getting back together again. Now, he visits my second husband and me (not often, as he lives abroad) and we all chat over a glass of wine. To me he feels like a distant relative that I'm vaguely fond of, but find quite irritating. It's a comfortable place to be. So if you can chat to your ex, I would. It will make the relationship easier and if nothing else, give you the moral high ground. That's not a bad place to be either.

7.1vii Craig, who is cautiously considering a new relationship...

For years, people had been advising me to leave him, or at least to radically change how I behaved if I was going to stay with him. 'Why do you put up with it?' was something I heard often, once someone had witnessed one of his sudden rages, when he would curse or insult or put me down in a way that I did not know how to respond to. I'd reason that they didn't understand: his criticisms were truly valid, and we were 'meant to be'. We would be together for life. I couldn't even contemplate not being at each other's side.

Then, one day, that tiny phrase came out of his mouth: 'It's over' – as shocking as a guillotine blade slicing my neck.

I wasn't having it, of course. I plotted how I could keep on being around him, and to a degree he seemed to cooperate (though the outbursts of abuse continued). Even as our connection was dying, we made elaborate plans to split the house physically (at least I'd get to see him, albeit not talk to him). We could add a basement and one of us could live in it.

I downloaded online courses on what to do when your partner claims to end your relationship, how not to panic, how not to 'give up' or 'lose hope'. I went on numerous meditation retreats (he was a Buddhist, surely he'd be impressed!) On one of these, a Zen master, a lovely, humorous, down-to-earth Welshman called Ken told me 'I see how you walk and how this relationship is dragging you down, you need to stand on your own two feet, to give yourself a chance!'

Ten months after he dumped me I finally admitted to myself I'd need to figure out how to extricate myself from this most 'uncivil' of civil partnerships.

Fast forward three more years – of bitter and costly warfare, much of it very public (and quite shaming) in front of solicitors and barristers and judges and bemused friends and relations –

and now I've got my life back. Or rather, my soul. I have started living – OK, at 57, 58 – but better that than never, right?

Every area of my life has been transformed for the better. Work. Health. Most of all, with the help of wonderful therapists (yes, plural – I don't believe in stinting myself!) I've tackled the sexual blocks that had blighted my whole life. I've been having fun with all sorts of gorgeous guys, often half my age! And recently I've met another man, a good-hearted man, a passionate, loving man, who tells me he wants to spend the rest of his life with me, and I'm cautiously, a bit warily, but perceptibly, allowing myself to fall for him. So maybe there's love at the end of that rainbow after all.

7.1viii Andrew, the dad who has found a way through

My story is one of hope! As I write this, I am currently in my ex's house, looking after our children, whilst she is on holiday with her new partner. I never thought I'd see the day. Our divorce was painfully long and deeply acrimonious. We both agreed that we should split, which may have made things easier on one level. There was no other person involved in our decision; we both just knew that we brought out the worst in each other. We'd been together about 16 years. Looking back, 95% of the bitterness and wrangling we went through was centred around our meagre finances. She'd come into the relationship with more than I had, and we had to divvy up the house. Still, in the end we were lucky – we didn't have to blow a large portion of it on legal fees.

After the divorce, for various reasons, my ex took our three children to live abroad. Given the distance, contact with them during this time was not particularly frequent. The first couple of years were very tough, and I spent a lot of time (and money) travelling to see them, renting a flat and car etc.

After this period of adjustment and settling into divorced life, my ex moved back to the UK. These days we don't do 'alternate weekends' – we never really have – and she spends most of the time looking after them, so she gets to pick when she sees them over the holidays. The result is new visiting arrangements and new boundaries; I have often stayed at her place and she has taken the opportunity to get away, generously letting me use her space. This has worked well for the children: they have not had to be shuffled around too much and they are still surrounded by their own things in familiar surroundings.

Increasingly, over time, she has chosen to stay at home whilst I've been visiting. We do things together. We both feel that the children benefit from us doing things 'as a family'. Until a couple of years ago, I had not spent Christmas day with my children since we'd split. Now we all spend Christmases together.

There are still lots of niggles, lots of triggers (we both know each other's tender spots). All those things that used to piss you off about your partner, those things that you tolerated because you were in love – when you split up, you no longer feel like you should tolerate them. But we still do for the sake of our children. All of these triggers are great lessons and opportunities for growth and self-improvement, if you allow them to be!

This is the first time in a while that she's been away on one of my visits and I couldn't be happier for her. She has a new relationship, and I too have a partner, and this is the first one where both my ex and my girlfriend get on. I can't tell you how much easier that is!

I have blustered my way through a lot of things in life and made a load of mistakes, but I'm fortunate that my relationship with my children is (fingers crossed) brilliant. I know that we made the right decision.

I'm blessed that things have turned out this way. My children seem incredibly well adjusted. Time together with them is sacred (at least to me). It is short, so there is very little time for a lot of the trifling matters that come up in normal families. We're just grateful to see each other and when we do, they get 100% of my attention. That seems key to a successful relationship with them.

Another thing that has worked for us, has been that we have always remained supportive of each other in front of the children.

The truth is: if we didn't have children together, I doubt our paths would ever cross now. But we DO have children together, and that bond will never change, so it's about making the best of that situation so that your life is not constantly filled with anguish and hatred, and about truly putting the children's interests first. That requires a different kind of sacrifice and tolerance to anything I've ever experienced! Our approach has worked in its own way... I hope this offers some light to those of you who are still struggling through the earlier phases of divorce – it can be done!

Finally... some considered advice: The person you divorced? *You loved them once.* I know horrible things may happen along the way, and things get complicated if you have children together, but you once loved each other. Cling on to that. Holding on to hatred and anger will slowly kill you. Only when you let go of that and can forgive each other (and yourself) will you properly heal. Only then will you shine again, and only then will you be ready and available for someone else.

7.2   Making a new life

So, it's over. You are officially no longer a couple and you have done all the tedious tasks that need doing. Now what? Perhaps you thought, after all the trauma and hard work of the split, that you would feel like celebrating. Some people do, and divorce parties are definitely a 'thing'. But I don't know anyone who has had one. The overwhelming feeling seems to be one of emptiness, sometimes laced with gloom. Now what? Where do you go from here?

You've received the decree absolute and with that, the relationship fizzles out (though there may be ongoing issues if you've children in common, and if you have not been able to achieve a clean break financially). Compared to the excitement and fanfare with which married life likely began (the culmination of plans involving special outfits, flowers and guestlists) the beginning of this new stage in your life can seem an anticlimax.

7.3 Reframing failure

People say 'my marriage failed'. Especially if the separation was forced upon you by your ex, it is easy to take that failure personally.

Divorce or the end of a long-term relationship is what David Sbarra (Professor of Psychology at the University of Arizona) calls a 'what now?' moment. A fork in the road, providing opportunities and obstacles for getting to the next level. A time to see our place in the world in new ways. His recipe for moving on includes:

- *Self compassion* – look at yourself as a dear friend would, accept your inadequacies and see your suffering as part of a common humanity, for example, 'I am not the first person to get divorced, nor the last'.
- *Self understanding* – divorce is an insult to our understanding of self, and can force us to examine 'who am I?' Sbarra says re-organising our sense of self is the engine that drives our self-healing and that we should pull our 'self' together.

TIP: Think of Kintsugi. Kintsugi, or 'golden joinery', is the centuries old Japanese art of repairing broken pottery with gold or other precious metals. The breakage and repair is treated as part of the history of the vessel, and celebrated rather than disguised. The ceramic is now stronger and more beautiful. Many people who have been scarred by a failed marriage (or other trauma) come to value the lessons learned in a similar way.

'There is a crack in everything. It's where the light gets in.'
Leonard Cohen

Use this opportunity for growth and self-improvement. Emotional pain has the potential to make us examine ourselves in a way we might never do when we are comfortable. Now is your chance to decide how to move forward. I think I can hear some of you complaining that everything has been taken from you and that the future holds nothing of worth. Not so. You may find, as I did, that your values change. For example, when I drive through my old neighbourhood now, what used to simply be 'home' reeks unpleasantly of privilege, and I see some of the concerns that I used to share with those who live there as a waste of energy.

'Start where you are, use what you have, do what you can.'
Arthur Ashe

I used to be a sanctimonious, smug married person. I thought people (including me and my ex) should try harder, stay together for the sake of the children etc. Now I am minded to think that many relationships run their course, and that our insistence on the idea of 'ever after' can be unhelpful, making us cling to things long after they've run their course.

Gary Lewandoski, another professor of psychology and relationship scientist, points out that 'Good relationships seldom fail. Bad ones do, as they should'. He says: 'When your relationship doesn't help you to become a better person, then ending it can.' My marriage did not help me to become a better person but my divorce did.

7.4 Working on pulling your 'self' together

I used to read about people who said things like 'I didn't know who I was any more' without comprehension. Now I know that twenty years in a partnership can mean that – like dogs and their owners – you come to resemble one another. I am ashamed to say that even some time after my ex left, and revealed himself not to be the brainbox I had imagined, I still sometimes fell into the trap of answering a question about what I thought with what I thought *he* thought. So, for example, it took me a while to find that I did not share his politics. It was not simply that I ignored signs that we may have been incompatible; rather, where we disagreed, I thought he must be right, and persuaded myself that I was wrong.

I now know it is not always as easy as it seems, to know what one thinks, what one likes. If you've always lacked confidence; if you have tended to put the needs of your other half and children before your own; if you have been mocked for your taste (in music, or whatever), or for your lack of education or intelligence – all this over the years can conspire to make you wonder what you really think or feel.

Have fun finding out! There are lots of good ways to do this, and you can try them all:

- Therapy
- Experimenting with new things
- Going back to old hobbies
- Meeting new people
- Rekindling relationships with people who knew you before

7.4i Therapy

Time is a great healer but it does not do all the work. We've talked a lot about the benefits of therapy elsewhere in the book. So I'll just say: if you are struggling to make sense of your relationship and its aftermath; if you are wondering what brought you and kept you together; if you are dealing with the realisation that you were deceived and feeling that your relationship was a sham; if fear of being hurt again is hampering your attempts to make new relationships; if you feel at all curious about how you ended up here, therapy can help.

> *'I normally cope really well with situations like this. I get my head down, get on with it and look to the future. But at some point I had to deal with my feelings. I went to some counselling sessions referred by my GP and within minutes I was in bits. All that pent up and hidden emotion came out and over eight sessions I became a new person. I'd recommend it to anyone going through a relationship breakdown. It really helped me.'* **Rose**

Divorce is difficult. You go through a lot of shit. Remember though, that appropriately used, shit can be a great fertilizer. Our shitty experience can help us flourish.

7.4ii Pursuing interests old and new

This is an opportunity to go back to things you used to enjoy, or to experiment with new ones, or both! So many of the things you did when young, or single, or before you had children, can get crowded out by things you have or choose to do later. Why not revisit them and see if they still excite you? Sports, art, singing. I went to a talk at the School of Life about ambition (which I sorely lack!) and found it mostly covered German philosophers. Back in the mists of time I studied German and Philosophy at university, and the sense of homecoming was a real treat.

> *'I used to love needlework but never had the time when married. Now I've joined a sewing circle and am enjoying the activity and the new friendships while making curtains for my new home.'* **Marianne**

> *'My ex was always very dismissive of my attempts to play the guitar. I've bought myself a new one, and am loving strumming along, writing songs and messing about in the evenings after work.'* **Jason**

TIP: Try Meetups[72]. They have groups for absolutely everything you can think of, so you can indulge your interests with people who share them. Art, pubs, IT, Spanish, theatre, walking, comedy, philosophy, dance, cooking, board games – you name it – and if you don't see what you are looking for, it's easy to start a group yourself.

Other than Meetups, try adult education classes to learn a new skill. These can be found all over the place, in colleges and schools and local community centres. You can take up car maintenance, crochet, computers...

'When I was first separated I realised I didn't know how to feed myself properly. I joined a local cookery class. I'm still friends with the people I met there, and we take turns to host dinners. I've gone on from that first class to more and more and now have quite a repertoire!' **Chris**

Why not volunteer? Local organisations are always looking for people to help, whether it's gardening in public spaces, reading to little ones in school, or making meals in homeless shelters. Helping others less fortunate than yourself is a great way to put your own problems into perspective and studies have shown that people who volunteer are happier than those who don't.

There is a book, 'Yes Man' by Danny Wallace, and a TED talk by Shonda Rhimes, with the same theme: they just decide to say yes to things they would normally have said no to and it opens up all kinds of opportunities. My default position has always tended to be 'No'. It's uncomfortable to force myself to say yes, but these days I do ('Pia, would you like to write a book about divorce?'). The rewards can be huge. Even when I have not liked something, I have been energised by the experience, and I have made a lot of friends along the way.

'It is impossible to live without failing at something, unless you live so cautiously that you might as well not have lived at all, in which case you have failed by default.' **J K Rowling**

7.4iii Having a social life

Many find that invitations dry up when they are newly single. And spending the evening curled up on the sofa alone doesn't have the same allure it had when you were a comfy twosome. If you've small children, and lost the default babysitter in your ex, maybe you are more tied to the house now than you were. And perhaps, financially, you're feeling the pinch. Then there is the possible lack of confidence to leave the house at all, the fear that you'll have nothing to say, or will burst into tears.

'I could no longer afford nights out with restaurants and theatre tickets. I think in the end some friends from my old life just found it less awkward not to ask.' **Thomas**

'Suddenly I was perceived as a threat to all the married men on the dinner party circuit and was out in the cold.' **Angelique**

You might think this can conspire to keep you from enjoying yourself and, after all, you may still be feeling a bit wobbly. Never fear! You can find other ways of enjoying your life, which may become more interesting and joyful than ever it was.

I used to give dinner parties, maybe a handful of couples from the children's schools. Three courses, seating plans… When my husband left and stopped providing any money at all for any of us or our home, I had to take in lodgers. Some of these have remained good friends and nowadays we regularly get together for themed dinners, to which we all contribute. We cook together and everyone mucks in. So much less stressful, less expensive, and more fun.

Re-connect with some of the people from your past; rekindle friendships that got neglected during your coupledom. I'm not just talking about hooking up with childhood sweethearts with a view to getting back together, but expanding your circle. I've loved making new friends, post separation, with people I might never normally have met. There is, however, a particular joy to be had from being with people who knew you 'before'. Facebook, LinkedIn etc make it easy to contact friends and acquaintances in a low-key way. Send a friendly message to say hello and see what happens. You never know. If nothing else, it's nice to touch base.

Sarah and I were old school friends who had lost touch when we went to separate universities thirty years ago and now look at us!

7.4iv To stay single or to try dating?

Some people relish being single again. After however many years of faithfulness, they are keen to explore the field and enjoy themselves. Others are terrified. It's been years. They feel fat or wrinkly. Worse, they feel rejected and unlovable. Personally speaking, I'm just not interested. I haven't been on a date since 1990, when I met my ex. And I wouldn't want to go on one now. I'm all for meeting people, though, and seeing old friends and new: the more the merrier! While I would not hesitate to go to the cinema alone if I felt like it, I get so much pleasure from being with others, and (having been reclusive for a long time) I am now making an effort to go out more, and reaping the rewards.

I may be unusual in this lack of interest in meeting a significant (or even insignificant) other, but there we are. At this stage in my life I am much more interested in cultivating my relationship with myself. And so far, it's going well. In fact, I think I may be 'the one'!

Nonetheless, some of you out there are bound to feel differently, so I'm handing over to Sarah, whose experience of dating is somewhat more recent than mine.

7.4v Meeting a significant other

Hello, dear readers. Whilst I'm remarried and Pia isn't, let me say from the off I do not believe replacing spouse number one (or two or three) with the next significant other is The Only Way True Happiness Lies. I do not. I spent many years in my twenties and thirties single and much of that time relished the experience. I danced on podiums in the Ministry of Sound, went on holidays with my girlfriends and attended umpteen weddings alone. I didn't meet my *first* husband until I was 38, and suffice it to say I kissed a lot of frogs, and fell for the odd worm before husband number one and I (briefly) wed. So what follows is not a rule book, or even a guide. It's simply a series of observations about dating, which I see as one of the many avenues open to you now. And let me be clear; it's ten years since I met my husband online, and Tinder (and Grindr and God knows what else) have come along since. The result is a faster-paced, more brutal dating environment than the one that existed when I was last putting myself out there. Nonetheless I *was* an 'early adopter' of online dating; I didn't just meet husband number two there, it's how I met husband number one as well. Should you at some point, maybe not now but in the future, wish to dip a toe in the dating pool again, here are your starters for 10.

7.4vi Where to meet someone

Joining a club or a class

- **The pros.** Learning/keeping fit/getting out – all these are good things for your mental and physical health. And if you don't meet the new love of your life, at least you are doing something you enjoy and possibly making new friends. Plus there won't be the same pressure of expectation you might feel going a more direct route.
- **The cons.** The odds of finding someone you fancy at a class? Low. The odds of them fancying you, too? Lower still. And being available? Probably about the same as a jackpot-winning lottery ticket. By all means join any class or club that appeals; this is a time to get out there, do things you wouldn't normally do and shake things up. Just don't expect Mr or Mrs Right to open an easel/be doing Zumba/shouting 'come on you Reds!' next to you.

Getting friends to introduce you

- **The pros.** You'll have an idea of whom you are meeting, which might make it less frightening. The odds of them being available – if your friends say they are – will be better.
- **The cons.** Again the odds of chemistry are slim. But yes, accept invitations to parties. (Accept invitations, full stop.)

Going through an agency

- **The pros.** These offer some kind of filter that the internet sites do not, and use people rather than algorithms.
- **The cons.** They often charge a lot of money. My divorce cost me tens of thousands of pounds. If you feel yours has cost you dear enough already too, forget going through an agency. If not, good luck!

Going online and using dating apps

- **The pros.** According to the *Telegraph*, there are 1400 internet dating sites and dating apps in the UK, catering for every imaginable peccadillo. With increasing popularity, all stigma has vanished. The UK's biggest sites – Match and E-Harmony – have over 3 million members apiece, so you certainly won't be short of choice. Moreover, online dating is not just a vehicle for the young. Whilst Tinder and other 'swipe'-based apps may have a younger profile, Huffington Post reports that the average age of a man looking for love online is 44, while women average 42 years old. With big players such as Saga involved too, middle age is clearly no cut-off. If you're interested, you may find the *Telegraph's* breakdown of the top 20 sites useful, and the Mirror's top 10 has a lot of overlap[73].

'The notion of going to a bar or club and picking someone up? I was in my mid-50s when I divorced, so frankly, no thank you. Mates' introductions were simply too few and far between – most of my friends were hooked up already, or gay (which I'm not). The main advantage to online dating is you know you are both looking – and there's a lot to be said for that. Some find it brutal, and it can be, so I did it in bursts – three months on, three months off. It took a while and initially I made some horrendous errors of judgement. But in the end, I met a good 'un. He wasn't the type I normally would have gone for physically, but I had a cancer scare and he handled it with such kindness, it made me look at him differently and give him a chance. I am so glad I did.' **Alexandra**

- **The cons.** Internet dating can be terrifying and if you are fresh from your separation, odds are you'll be vulnerable. There are plenty of people, unfortunately, who prey on those who come blinking into the dating scene looking for love. Even if you don't fall into the hands of the unscrupulous, you may be hurt by one or two of the other people out there, who might be similarly escaping from their own painful past. Plus things will have changed since you were last on the dating scene; if you were with your ex a long time, they may have changed hugely.

FACT: Approximately one in four meet their spouse at work.

FACT: Approximately one in four relationships start online[74].

So if you don't see a potential Significant Other loitering at the water cooler, it stands to reason your next best bet is going online.

'I found it great for my confidence and it was nice to meet women I had things in common with.' **Andy**

'My marriage broke down after my husband had an affair, so I had a "revenge fuck" with a guy I met on Tinder. It was meaningless but what's the problem with that? Neither of us got hurt and it got something out of my system.' **Edie**

'It's easy to get stuck in the rut of singledom, especially if your self-esteem is low. When Pat and I broke up, I spent months imagining all sorts of things that he and his new partner were getting up to. It was agony. Then I went online, and met a guy. We hooked up a few times and it didn't work out, and I came out a bit bruised, so I've put dating on hold for the moment. I'm OK though – it's not like we'd declared undying love or anything and I didn't sleep with him – though I'd have liked to. What was good was it helped stop me from hankering after Pat. I may go back to it, or I may not.' **Marie**

Internet Dating Pointers

'Last week I separated from my husband. I'm already seeing someone new and he is absolutely amazing! He has shown me how a real man should treat a woman.' **Cheryl**

Like me and Pia, you might wince at the naiveté of the post above, which appeared on a divorce site recently. 'Isn't it wise not to hurtle headlong from one relationship to another without taking stock?' you might say and, on the whole, I'd agree. But we each have to find our own way, and there's something to be said for getting back on the proverbial horse that threw you off, and learning through experience what you want – what type of person might suit you or whether a relationship suits you at all.

Here are some lessons I learned:

- After my first marriage broke up, a wise and honest friend said to me, 'Perhaps what you think is a good match for you *isn't*. After all, it hasn't worked so far.' I looked at my 44-year-old self and thought, 'Hmm, yes, she has a point'. So I'd pass this advice on. **Try to overcome your prejudices and look beyond the restrictions you put on potential suitors in the past.**
  - If you've always gone for those who like to live in the fast lane, then maybe you might look for someone who is aware of speed cameras.
  - If your spouse supported you financially but it left you undervaluing your self-worth, then consider someone who'll support your striving for independence.
  - If you've tended to value physical beauty very highly, you could consider whether someone who makes you laugh might be more attractive in the long term.

And so on. Let me illustrate. I'm a writer and I like someone who can string a sentence together. So when Tom first emailed me and his message was full of typos and poor spelling, I nearly cast him aside. Which would have

165

been my loss. ('Damn right!' he says from the sofa.) When I met him, I discovered he was warm and witty and we had a lot in common. But I could easily have never discovered that, if I'd made a snap decision based on very little at all. Which leads me on to…

- **Keep an open mind.** It's tempting, if we've been badly burned, to come out thinking *all* men are bastards, *all* women are harpies and so on. Neither of these is true, and just because you've been involved in one relationship car crash doesn't mean you're destined for another. I was fortunate in that my parents both remarried, and happily, after their own divorce. Through them I learned it was quite possible to meet someone nice and kind and to whom you are better suited even after gravity and middle-aged spread have begun to take their toll. Be wary, by all means, and protect your tender heart. But one bad apple does not spoil the whole bunch of guys and girls.

- You may have to try, try, try again but **please don't be disheartened**. It's not a reflection of *you* but of the chemistry between you, albeit sometimes only for an hour or two. And awful dates can make excellent anecdotes or learning experiences, so even a bad hook-up can prove better than staying in alone.

- **Shared interests matter.** You don't need to like all the same things – far from it – but if you think someone's taste is *awful* when you meet them, it will probably grate much more after a while. Liking similar music, having political opinions that are in sync, a passion for travel – these can help oil the wheels of a relationship and allow you to overcome differences as and when they (inevitably) emerge. It's for good reason you'll be asked for these details by most major dating sites.

- **Get someone else to choose your profile picture**; better still, if you're straight, ask someone of the opposite sex to choose; if you're gay, get a gay friend to. I was poised to post a picture of me looking what I thought was sexy. My friend John hooted on seeing it. 'You can't put that!' 'Why

166

not?' I asked. 'You're pouting,' he said. 'And it doesn't look like you anyway.' Together he and another mate chose the picture that eventually attracted Tom. I was smiling and looked 'like Sarah', they said.

- **Show, don't tell**. My sister-in-law asked my husband what attracted him to my profile. 'She was funny,' he said (amongst other things). 'Other women banged on about what a great sense of humour they had, but her profile actually made me laugh.' So, don't simply *say* you have a GSOH (the world and his ex-wife does that). Show it.

- **Don't ask for the earth.** Think of the person reading your profile and how it might make them feel if you make too many demands. You don't want to put off a lovely person who *doesn't* earn £100K a year, do you? (Maybe you do, but then you've a different set of values to me, and my advice probably won't help you.)

*'What some people say they want in a partner is really off-putting. I'd read these profiles and think, "I don't earn **that** much, I don't own my own property and I'm not over 6', so no point going there". Women who felt they'd been shafted over money then looked for a richer guy for instance, instead of looking for someone who was trustworthy. Women who were disappointed ended up with a bigger set of demands, rather than a **different** set of demands which might have suggested they'd learned from their experience. On more than one occasion, I started an email conversation and then found the woman was still angry, and her rage would emerge in digs at me. What these women wanted may not have been unreasonable, but I wasn't responsible for their marital breakdown and didn't like being made to feel I was.'* **Len**

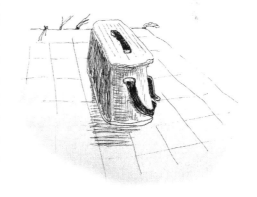

When writing what sort of partner you're after, by all means say what you'd like in a person, but **be realistic**. If you've kids and baggage, then it's only fair to make room for both in return.

*'Sarah didn't really fit my profile – I have a son and he was only eight at the time, so I thought what would be best was someone who had children and who understood the demands of having one. And my vanity led me to assume I'd be well matched to someone who was younger. But neither turned out to be what suited me. I read Sarah's profile and thought, "I'm going to like this person" and so that over-rode those other things – and we arranged to meet. So what you **think** you want, and what you **actually** want, are not necessarily the same. We got on. We made each other laugh. But we knew – and this is the beauty of internet dating – that we had common ground. Sarah studied at Leeds, I was from Bradford, we liked the same music and shared similar politics, and that made it worth pursuing. Whilst it's good to have an idea of what's important to you in another person, you can't be completely rigid about it because there's a chemistry and you don't know where it's going to come from.'* **Tom**

Dating can be a good way to get to know yourself better.

'When I was first divorced I lurched from one unsuitable relationship to another. It took a few years and a long hard look at myself before I stopped attracting the wrong sort. Right now I am single, happy that way, and open to meeting someone if the right person turns up.' **Elsa**

Don't lie. If you are not yet divorced, say so.

'Age, weight, jobs... They lie about everything and put completely fake pics up. There was one guy who talked about his ex all night and ended up in tears.' **Jack**

FACT: 1/3 of people admit to lying about themselves in their online profile[75]. Don't be one of them.

Internet dating can be an emotional minefield and at times, dangerous. If you plan to try it, **please do your utmost to stay safe**.

Staying safe online dating

- Take it slow. Some sites, especially those aimed at casual hook-ups, can resemble cattle markets: people tend to be on them for one thing only, and many may be married.
- Beware anyone coming on too strong.
- Be on your guard. It is easy for people to disguise their true identities and, after all, they are perfect strangers.
- Be very cautious about giving identifying information like your home address.
- Before meeting, chat on the phone (voice, not text) and ideally, on a landline. This will give you a better idea who you are dealing with.
- Meet the first time for coffee in a public place.
- Tell a friend where you are going and when you will be back.
- Check some of the useful advice online eg Wikihow about how to spot date scammers – this includes using Google search to see if profile pictures appear elsewhere.
- Do not send money![76]
- Trust your instinct.

Have fun, be safe, and let us know in Making Peace with Divorce on Facebook how you get on.

And now, it's back to Pia…

7.5 Holidays

TIP: Think about holidaying with friends, strangers or alone.

If you have the money and the time, don't think you can't go on holiday just because you no longer have a partner. You may find that your circle of friends has changed and includes some other singles who might want to go with you. A few years ago a friend of mine booked an activity holiday on the spur of the moment with one of many companies that specialises in holidays for singles, came back with a handful of good friends she still sees and has booked further solo holidays.

I've had few holidays since the split and have taken my children, but I have also travelled a little alone and I can't tell you how rewarding it was. Making my own way places, not having anyone else to talk to or please en route after all those years of shepherding children and negotiating with my ex. Bliss. It made me feel young again. I made my way through the airport and saw fractious families, bored or bickering. I thought 'that used to be us'. Staying in a hotel alone, like I used to on business before kids, meant I saw more. I looked around. I talked to strangers. It was lovely. Time and money permitting, I would like to travel more, maybe join one of those holidays where you learn to paint or improve your tennis.

TIP: You probably have friends you could visit, dotted all over the globe.

If you have small children, it can be hard taking them on holiday as a single parent, but there are ways to ease things: you could go with another family, or to a place with activities to keep children busy. And if there are times when your children are away with your ex, use that time for yourself, whether home or abroad.

7.6 Festivities

Christmas time and other big events in the calendar can be awkward after a split and feel very lonely. But, while the first few in particular may be painful, it does get better. Especially if you take steps to look after yourself.

When my ex left, I no longer had to have his whole extended family over to stay. The kids and I decided that we never liked turkey anyway, and now enjoy a goose, which is plenty for a smaller crowd, and (we think) tastier.

TIP: Rather than try to recreate the spirit of Christmases past, think about making some new traditions.

Some newly divorced friends I know get together with others who will be alone and find that, as with so many things, different is not necessarily worse. To be with a bunch of mates (each possibly with their own family Christmas memories playing in the back of their heads) can feel strange. Or it can provide comfort and support. Some are not up to it and retreat to their bed for the day for a spot of wallowing and simply pleasing themselves. There are usually good movies on…

'I was worried about my first Xmas on my own, so I booked myself a holiday in Thailand. It was strange but interesting.' **Charles**

Alternatively, how about volunteering in a homeless shelter or doing something for others? I remember how, suddenly, I saw the supermarket displays for Xmas – and Valentine's – in a different light. I realised that in previous years I had given barely a thought to the people who were newly divorced, or bereaved, or homeless as I went about my business looking for stocking fillers or celebratory meals. It can seem as though you are the only one who is missing out, but you know that there are many who are worse off than you, and helping others can boost mood and a sense of wellbeing. And remember, the time of festivities is famously stressful even in happy families. If you are now having to negotiate with exes, and make new traditions because you no longer have in-laws to visit, or because your children will be spending some of the time with the other parent, try to be glass half-full about it, not half empty.

7.7 Looking on the bright side

TIP: Make a list of positives about your new situation. And there are some.

We tend to focus on what we miss. What *don't* you miss? To start you off, here are some positives I have heard from others – things people enjoy now that they are no longer in a couple. You might recognise some as benefits of your own.

> *'I don't miss my ex snoring, and as for farting – I used to have to tie the duvet down.'* **Ginny**

- Being able to wear what I like
- Not having to spend time with my in-laws
- Not having to walk on eggshells
- Eating what I like, when I like
- My bedroom, with new girly fabrics
- Having the bed to myself without my wife throwing the duvet on and off

- Not having to have sex when I don't want to
- Time to myself when the children are with my ex
- Not having to tell anyone where I am or when I will be back
- Knowing how much money is in the bank
- Not being lied to

You may be able to create your own list. If it helps, put it on the door of the fridge to remind you each day. I know this may sound odd, but I think that being miserable can become a comforting normality and if you find yourself falling into this trap, expecting the worst, and greeting each new set-back as inevitable, do make a conscious effort to notice positives.

'And I urge you to please notice when you are happy, and exclaim or murmur or think at some point, "If this isn't nice, I don't know what is".' **Kurt Vonnegut**

Not that they haven't also heard me cry or moan over the last few years, sometimes almost interminably, and not that I don't still do it now, but my children are also getting used to hearing me say 'If this isn't nice, I don't know what is'.

If you can't help being reminded of them, maybe make a list of the things you *do* miss. Is there a way you can get some of these things back? At the risk of sounding nauseatingly Pollyanna-ish (you may remember the book in which Pollyanna sought 'reasons to be glad' in misfortunes) I would suggest it is a good exercise to see if you can find positives in any given situation.

'When I haven't any blue I use red.' **Pablo Picasso**

TIP: If you miss cuddles and affection, try doling them out to friends and family – or your pet!

I find I sometimes miss cooking for a larger family so from time to time I invite people round. Win win. I miss my old home, which was centrally located and, after many years of improvements, was finally the way I wanted it. There is no getting away from the fact that my new home is less than 20% of the value of the old for a reason, and I don't like being so far away and living with someone else's kitchen. However, my move has its upsides:

- I've got to know a new part of town
- I've made new friends in this neighbourhood
- The previous owners – not gardeners – left me a clean slate and my son and I have enjoyed ourselves enormously in creating a beautiful new space to our own taste
- Even the extremely painful process of shedding the contents of a large family home and having to sell valuables and sentimental mementos has been liberating and left me less encumbered with *stuff*
- I've proved to myself that I can make complicated financial decisions without my husband
- To my surprise I find living without a home alarm system much less stressful

And if anniversaries are a problem, see if these can't be reframed, too. A friend who can't forget the day her ex left her has chosen to refer to it as 'Freedom Day'. She makes sure to celebrate the day with some low-key pleasant activity so that the good memories will swamp the bad.

7.8 Looking forward and back

In the wake of divorce it can be easy to feel hard done by, broken hearted or angry. Being dumped, deceived or abused – whatever led to where we are now – the loss of our partner, the upset to children and the wider family, the loss of money, status, home. I would like to argue in favour of a two-pronged approach to getting out of negative emotions so that you are not bitter, angry or sad for the rest of your life.

Look back. Mull over your mistakes. Work out where you went wrong. Yes, you. Not your ex. I've said throughout this book that I am a fan of therapy and it certainly comes in handy here. Why did you choose the partner you did? What made you put up with a bad relationship or blind to its faults? What made you cling to the status quo? Once you own your part in your relationship breakdown, it is much easier to move confidently forward (whether into a new relationship or not).

> *'The truth will set you free. But first it will piss you off.'*
> **Gloria Steinem**

If you get involved with someone else, it should be from a position of strength, not neediness. You should not *need* a partner so much as *enjoy* someone to share things with. It will make your relationships more rewarding. It will also make you more attractive.

175

I once heard someone on the radio define love 'as a meeting of two pathologies'. It may lack romance but I think there is something in that. We tend to find a partner whose limitations fit our own. Therefore it stands to reason, the better we know ourselves and learn from our mistakes, the less likely we are to make them again on the rebound with partners of a similar type, who will likely hurt us in similar ways. Therapy or counselling of various types can help, and an experienced practitioner can help us to see things about ourselves that we have been blind to. Importantly, they can also help us to love ourselves in spite of these mistakes or weaknesses.

7.9 Conclusion – living happily

'New beginnings are often disguised as painful endings.' **Lao Tzu**

I know some people can divorce relatively painlessly, even amicably, but this book is not really aimed at them. They will likely have no need of it. Their breakup might just be a breakup. I have exes with whom I get on well and who did not break my heart. My divorce was different. I was completely broken. I was traumatised and helpless. It's easy to think that the degree of hurt is a measure of how good things were. I realise now that the opposite may be closer to the truth. My utter dependence on my husband was a symptom of and maybe even part of the reason that my marriage was not good.

Do you know the story of the frog in the pot? If you put a frog into a pot of boiling water, it jumps out. But if you put it into cold water and then heat it gradually, the frog, apparently, boils to death. I think my husband and I were both frogs in an uncomfortably hot pot, and in the end he jumped out. I don't blame him for that. I can even forgive him for (some of) the terrible, foolish lies and stealing during our marriage.

'Let go or be dragged.' **Zen proverb**

In a novel by Ernest Hemingway I believe someone is described as going bankrupt 'very slowly, and then all at once.' The end of my marriage went very slowly, all at once, and very slowly again. I did not see it clearly at the time, but my marriage was a cage in which we were both imprisoned. I am enormously grateful to him for breaking out of the prison himself and thus freeing me from it.

When I was married I was anxious and unhappy to the point of brittleness. Yet it did not occur to me to leave my husband; I thought we should change and improve things within the marriage. I clung to the familiarity of my marriage even though it made us both unhappy. It was worse than lack of nerve (though I did lack nerve): I lacked the imagination. It did not occur to me. People have asked me since, why did I not leave him? At the time I stared uncomprehending and said, 'Why would I leave him? I love him!' I can see now, despite all the heartache and upset, that it would have been better for us to have separated sooner (or arguably never married at all, if not for the fact that I would be without my children) and I am grateful that he never came back despite my entreaties.

'Someone I loved once gave me a box full of darkness. It took me years to understand that this too, was a gift.' **Mary Oliver, poet**

Aside from forgiving him, there are also things I have to forgive myself for. Like not asserting myself, not wanting to believe uncomfortable things, and lashing out in fear. I'm recognising that we both did what we could, given our own limitations. There's an element of sorrow and an element of making amends. I am learning to make peace with my marriage, my separation, my ex and myself. I think it is making me wiser and more comfortable in my skin than when I was married. I hope so.

'The privilege of a lifetime is to become who you truly are.' **Carl Jung**

When my husband first left me, a friend who had recently been through divorce passed on some advice. 'When you suddenly find yourself in deep water, your instinct is to paddle back as fast as possible to the shore from which you lost your footing. Tread water for a while,' she suggested. 'Survey the scene. There may be better places to swim to.'

My story is also a story of hope. And it's not over. I may not be there yet, but I'm still swimming.

JOIN THE CONVERSATION

'Never doubt that a small group of thoughtful, committed citizens can change the world. Indeed, it is the only thing that ever has.'
Margaret Mead

Time and again throughout this book we've heard others say that talking about what you're experiencing can lighten the load and increase understanding, and hearing from others who've been through something similar can provide reassurance that you're not alone. Sarah and I hope that's part of what this book, *Making Peace with Divorce*, with its interjections and insights from many throughout, has given you.

If you'd like to continue the conversation yourself, why not join the **Facebook group** we've often mentioned? **www.facebook.com/ groups/makingpeacewithdivorce** is the place to go in order to share tips and seek advice from others too.

If you'd prefer not to, that's fine. Sarah and I would like to end by saying **thank you** for reading, and good luck with your separation and beyond.

Note
We have aimed to be as thorough in our fact checking as possible but things still slip through despite sharp eyes. Do let us know if there is something important missing or wrong. Bear in mind that websites, correct today, may be absent tomorrow.

ACKNOWLEDGEMENTS

The most obvious person to thank is Sarah, for asking me to write this book in the first place and then being such a pleasure to work with. You gave me yet another experience I might never have enjoyed had I not been forced out of my comfort zone. Thank you.

Karen Chapman, my divorce lawyer, was kind enough to read the book and suggest where I needed to clarify points of law. If you're looking for a warm and sensible family solicitor with an eye for detail and a sense of humour, look no further: Google her name.

I am indebted to all the men and women, friends and strangers, who contributed their thoughts and experiences to the many examples quoted here. I have been privileged to learn from all of you. Laura Wilkinson and Leigh Forbes, thank you for your work in getting this book into shape.

My old friends are worth their weight in gold. I have been blessed as well with many new, some of whom started as supportive correspondents on Wikivorce and are now amongst my most treasured confidants. I owe more than thanks to friends and family for their support over the last few years – especially for my children's love and forbearance. I really needed it while unwittingly gathering material for this book. And now (they will likely be pleased to hear) I'd like to turn my mind to other subjects!

ENDNOTES

1. *Making Friends* series: sarah-rayner.com.
2. Office of National Statistics 2014.
3. **Counselling and psychotherapy – what are the differences?**
   Please note that although the terms counselling and therapy are often used interchangeably, there are differences between the two. The term counselling generally refers to a short-term consultation while psychotherapy typically refers to longer-term treatment. Counselling might reference your past, but counselling's focus is usually on helping you with what you are experiencing right now.

   Should you have counselling, you will tend to decide with your counsellor during the first meeting how many sessions you will have together, which can be anywhere from 12 to 24 weeks or more. Because it's shorter term, counselling can be quite structured, with an agenda laid out in advance.

   Psychotherapy looks at your behavioural patterns that are causing you distress in your daily life too, but in addition will work to help you have a deep understanding of your emotions by looking at your past. It questions how what you experienced as a child and young adult affected you in ways that might still be causing you issues now. There are many kinds of therapists (Freudian, Jungian, Psychodynamic etc). Therapy sessions may be less chatty – my therapist barely opened her mouth so that at first I wondered what the point of her was and felt that I could equally well sit at home and talk to myself. It took some months before I got an inkling that I was starting to listen to myself differently. But if you feel you would like more interaction, there are psychotherapists who work that way too.

   Whether you opt for counselling or therapy, do make sure you consult an accredited professional. The two main professional bodies are bacp.co.uk and psychotherapy.org.uk.
4. wikivorce.com
5. huffingtonpost.com/jill-brooke/for-those-getting-married_b_278186.html
6. The actual exception that proves the rule: a ruling in a UK court in 2017 caused outrage and national headlines when appeal judges found for the husband, who refuted his wife's grounds for divorce. This is unbelievably rare, indeed I doubt we will ever see such a thing again. (Some guidelines for suitable grounds for divorce – see chapter 5)

7. amhc.org/58-grief-bereavement-issues/article/8444-stage-of-grief-models-kubler-ross.
8. facebook.com/groups/MakingPeaceWithDivorce/
9. David Sbarra's TED talk: youtube.com/watch?v=vg92QEL4w4I
10. Al Anon Family Groups, for families & friends: al-anonuk.org.uk
11. nhs.uk/Conditions/stress-anxiety-depression/Pages/controlling-anger.aspx
12. huffingtonpost.com/megan-devine/stages-of-grief_b_4414077.html
13. amazon.co.uk/Making-Friends-Anxiety-supportive-little-ebook/dp/B00N2R85QY
14. alexandertechnique.co.uk
15. psychologytoday.com/blog/shame/201305/the-difference-between-guilt-and-shame
16. huffingtonpost.com/2012/09/19/your-money-what-can-a-div_n_1897963.html
    huffingtonpost.com/jason-levoy/5-reasons-you-need-a-divo_b_9278890.html
17. sortingoutseparation.org.uk
18. gingerbread.org.uk
19. wikivorce.com
20. facebook.com/groups/MakingPeaceWithDivorce/
21. It is not quite as cut and dried as this, especially for wealthier couples. Everything accumulated during the marriage goes into the marital pot, and if the needs of both parties can be met from these resources, the arguments about isolating assets acquired prior to the relationship do carry some weight. In the recent case of Hart v Hart, it was noted that 'the sharing principle applies with force to marital property. However it does not apply or applies with considerably less force, to non-marital assets'. Therefore, if you owned something prior to marriage and kept it in your sole name, and if both parties' needs can be met from resources built up during the marriage, then you may have a stronger case for keeping it out of the pot.
22. In the case of Miller v MacFarlane (2006), Lord Nicholls stated:
    "In the case of a short marriage, fairness may well require that the claimant should not be entitled to a share of the other's non-matrimonial property. The source of the asset may be a good reason for departure from equality. This reflects the instinctive feeling that the parties will generally have less call upon each other on the breakdown of a short marriage".
23. Note that the law in Scotland is different: gifts and inheritances do not form part of the marital property.
24. thecreditagency.co.uk/experian/financial-disassociation.pdf
    thecreditagency.co.uk/equifax/equifax-notice-of-disassociation.pdf
    thecreditagency.co.uk/callcredit/financial-disassociation.pdf

25. STI: Sexually Transmitted Infection
26. gov.uk/inherits-someone-dies-without-will/y/england-and-wales/yes/yes/no
27. If you have children, the first £250k and all personal possessions (whatever their value) passes to the spouse. Half the remainder also goes to the spouse, the other half is distributed equally to any children. See: gov.uk/inherits-someone-dies-without-will/y/england-and-wales/yes – for more information about intestacy.
28. gov.uk/power-of-attorney/overview
29. theguardian.com/lifeandstyle/2015/nov/22/children-divorce-resolution-survey-rather-parents-separate
30. rcpsych.ac.uk/healthadvice/parentsandyouthinfo/parentscarers/divorceorseparation.aspx
31. cafcass.gov.uk/media/190788/parenting_plan_final_web.pdf
32. cmoptions.org
33. cafcass.gov.uk/media/266763/drs_spip_dispute_resolution_services_directory_2016-17_1.pdf
34. cmoptions.org/index.asp
35. cnvc.org
36. divorcedmoms.com/blogs/thriving-in-crazy-land/how-do-to-coparent-with-an-abusive-ex
37. 'Why I unfriended my soon-to-be ex-husband – and all our mutual friends, too' https://goodmenproject.com/featured-content/why-i-unfriended-my-soon-to-be-ex-husband-and-all-our-friends-too-fiff/
38. facebook.com/notes/creative-pumpkin-publishing/stepparenting/375202332916617/
39. gov.uk/legal-separation
40. gov.uk/divorce/file-for-divorce
41. Except in the unlikely event that the divorce is contested, in which case the final hearing would be heard in open court.
42. marilynstowe.co.uk/2016/03/31/pitfalls-for-the-litigant-in-person/
43. wikivorce.com/divorce/Divorce-Advice/Self-Representation/281815-Tips-for-self-repping.html
44. mckenzie-friend.org.uk
45. chambersandpartners.com
46. resolution.org.uk
47. rightsofwomen.org.uk/get-information/family-law/family-law-legal-aid/
48. rightsofwomen.org.uk/wp-content/uploads/2014/10/PDF-guide-to-Family-Law-Legal-Aid.pdf
49. barprobono.org.uk
50. citizensadvice.org.uk
51. lawcentres.org.uk
52. sortingoutseparation.org.uk/legal-mediation/getting-free-legal-advice/#I0fmY

53. childrenslegalcentre.com/get-legal-advice/child-and-family/
54. relate.org.uk/relationship-help/help-separation-and-divorce
55. deborahnelsonfamilylaw.co.uk/useful-templates
moneyanddivorce.co.uk/2013/06/preparing-your-documents-for-first.html
56. This example copied from the Intelligent Divorce website: moneyanddivorce.co.uk/2013/06/preparing-your-documents-for-first.html - useful source of info
57. justice.gov.uk/courts/procedure-rules/family/practice_directions/pd_part_27a
58. justice.gov.uk/courts/procedure-rules/family/practice_directions/pd_part_22a
59. hmctsformfinder.justice.gov.uk/HMCTS/GetForm.do?court_forms_id=2655
60. justice.gov.uk/courts/procedure-rules/family/practice_directions/pd_part_12b
61. gov.uk/looking-after-children-divorce/after-you-apply-for-a-court-order
62. cafcass.gov.uk
63. gingerbread.org.uk/factsheet/19/Parental-responsibility-
64. hmctsformfinder.justice.gov.uk/HMCTS/GetForm.do?court_forms_id=2253
65. familycourtinfo.org.uk/i-need/how-court-works/flowchart-for-child-arrangements-cases/
66. cafcass.gov.uk/about-cafcass/national-commissioning-team/child-contact-interventions.aspx
67. hmctsformfinder.justice.gov.uk/HMCTS/GetForm.do?court_forms_id=2252
68. hmctsformfinder.justice.gov.uk/HMCTS/GetLeaflet.do?court_leaflets_id=1045
69. courttribunalfinder.service.gov.uk/search/
70. marilynstowe.co.uk/2015/01/22/enforcing-contact-orders/
71. formfinder.hmctsformfinder.justice.gov.uk/d50k-eng.pdf
72. meetup.com
73. mirror.co.uk/money/top-10-online-dating-websites-5220768
telegraph.co.uk/women/sex/the-20-best-online-dating-websites/
74. theguardian.com/lifeandstyle/2009/jan/24/dating-statistics
75. theguardian.com/lifeandstyle/2009/jan/24/dating-statistics
76. wikihow.com/Spot-an-Online-Dating-Scammer

USEFUL WEBSITES

Divorce support
facebook/groups/makingfriendswithdivorce
wikivorce.com
sortingoutseparation.org.uk
gingerbread.org.uk
gov.uk – useful information about all aspects of separation
al-anonuk.org.uk – if your life has been affected by someone's drinking
freedomprogramme.co.uk – if you have been in an abusive relationship
gov.uk/stop-forced-marriage – government site with information and sources of support for forced marriages
supportline.org.uk/problems/forced_marriages.php – lists a number of sources of support with forced marriages

Legal
chambersandpartners.com
hmctsformfinder.justice.gov.uk
mckenzie-friend.org.uk
resolution.org.uk
rightsofwomen.org.uk
barprobono.org.uk
citizensadvice.org.uk
lawcentres.org.uk
justice.gov.uk
courttribunalfinder.service.co.uk

Mediation
familymediationcouncil.org.uk/find-local-mediator/
resolution.org.uk/find_a_mediator/
thefma.co.uk/find-a-mediator-near-you/

Financial
thecreditagency.co.uk/experian/financial-disassociation.pdf
thecreditagency.co.uk/equifax/equifax-notice-of-disassociation.pdf
thecreditagency.co.uk/callcredit/financial-disassociation.pdf
moneysavingexpert.com

Counselling
relate.org.uk
bacp.co.uk
psychotherapy.org.uk

Mental health
mhf.org.uk
mind.org.uk
moodscope.com
actionforhappiness.org
sane.org.uk
time-to-change.org.uk

Children
cafcass.gov.uk
cmoptions.org
childrenslegalcentre.com
familycourtinfo.org

Social and dating
meetups.com
match.com
eharmony.co.uk

RECOMMENDED READING

Runaway husbands by Vikki Stark

The Curse of Lovely by Jacqui Marson

Codependent No More by Melody Beattie

The Happiness Project by Gretchen Rubin

The Family Law A-Z by Nick and Ruth Langford

How to talk so children will listen, and listen so children will talk by Adele Faber and Elaine Mazlish

Fiction
For a long time I could not concentrate on reading a single paragraph, and gave up reading fiction altogether. As I have recovered I have rediscovered my love of fiction and I have found the insights into character and relationship in novels very valuable, maybe more so than anything else I have read. I would say these are likely to be found in any good literature that has relationships as its subject. Lately I have enjoyed the novels of Charles Dickens, Richmal Crompton, Dorothy Whipple, Elizabeth Taylor, Arnold Bennett, Rachel Cusk... too many to list.

Making Friends with Anxiety:
A warm, supportive little book to help ease worry and panic

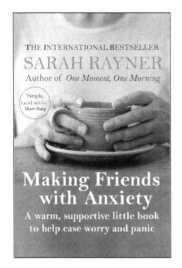

'Simple, lucid advice on how to accept your anxiety' **Matt Haig, bestselling author of** *Reasons to Stay Alive.*

Drawing on her experience of **anxiety disorder and recovery**, Sarah Rayner explores this common and often distressing condition with candour and humour. She reveals **the seven elements that commonly contribute to anxiety** including adrenaline, negative thinking and fear of the future, and explains why it becomes such a problem for many of us. **Packed with tips and exercises** and offset by the author's photographs and anecdotes from her life, if you suffer from panic attacks, a debilitating disorder or just want to reduce the amount of time you spend worrying, *Making Friends with Anxiety* will give you a greater understanding of how your mind and body work together, helping restore confidence and control.

- Uses **Mindfulness-based Cognitive Therapy** techniques
- Includes **photographs** by the author to lift the spirit
- **Useful links** throughout, plus details of **helplines** and **recommended reads**
- Online support available – share experiences and tips with over 7000 members

'Reads like chatting with an old friend; one with wit, wisdom and experience' **Laura Lockington, Brighton and Hove Independent**

Making Friends with Your Fertility
A clear and comforting guide to reproductive health

'A must read... A robust, resilient friend for everyone considering their fertility and an essential addition to any fertility professional's bookshelf.' **Susan Seenan, Chief Executive, Fertility Network UK**

From the onset of periods and puberty, through egg and sperm production and preparing to conceive naturally, to IVF and assisted conception, in *Making Friends with your Fertility*, counsellor Tracey Sainsbury and bestselling author Sarah Rayner them all with warmth and humour. Together they take you on a journey not just exploring what happens when things go well (through intercourse, orgasm and pregnancy), but also looking at situations where conception is not so straightforward, as it isn't for 1 in 6 heterosexual couples experiencing infertility or for those who are single or in same sex relationships and keen to have a baby. And *Making Friends with your Fertility* is not just for those trying to conceive – it's for all those keen to support them – friends and family, counsellors and healthcare professionals too.

The result is a handy, practical primer that makes these complex and sometimes distressing issues less confusing and overwhelming, supporting each individual with sensitivity and honesty so they can 'make friends' with their own fertility, in whatever form that takes.

Making Friends with the Menopause:
A clear and comforting guide to support you as your body changes
2017 edition reflecting the new 'NICE' guidelines

Written with Sarah Rayner's trademark warmth and humour, this **new edition of the popular** *Making Friends with the Menopause* **has been updated to reflect the latest National Institute for Health and Care guidelines on diagnosis and management of the menopause**. Together with Dr Patrick Fitzgerald, she explores why stopping menstruating causes such profound chemical changes in the body, leading us to react in a myriad of ways physically and mentally. There is practical advice on hot flushes and night sweats, anxiety and mood swings, muscular aches and loss of libido, early-onset menopause, hysterectomy and more, plus a simple explanation of each stage of the menopause so you'll know what to expect. You'll find details of the treatment options available, together with tips and insights from women keen to share their wisdom. Whether you're worried about feeling invisible, weight gain or loss of fertility, or simply want to take care of yourself well, knowledge is power, and *Making Friends with the Menopause* will give you a greater understanding of the process, so you can enjoy your body and your sexuality as you age.

- Includes advice on all the major health issues that can arise as a result of hormone change
- Includes traditional and complementary medicine
- Gives guidance on how to get the most from your GP appointments and finding good alternative practitioners
- Useful links throughout, plus details of helplines and recommended reads

Making Friends with Depression:
A warm and wise companion to recovery

From the bestselling authors of *Making Friends with Anxiety* and *The 5/2 Diet Book* comes a clear and comforting book to help sufferers of depression.

If you're suffering very low mood, you can end up feeling very alone, desperately struggling to find a way through, but recovery *is* possible and Sarah Rayner and Kate Harrison, together with Dr Patrick Fitzgerald show you how. They explain that hating or fighting the 'black dog' of depression can actually prolong your suffering, whereas 'making friends' with your darker emotions by compassionately accepting these feelings can restore health and happiness.

Sarah and Kate write with candour, compassion and humour because they've both been there and, together with Dr Patrick Fitzgerald, have produced a concise and practical guide to help lift low mood and support the journey to recovery. It explains:

- The different types of depressive illness
- Where to seek help and how to get a diagnosis
- The pros and cons of the most common medications
- The different kinds of therapy available
- Why depression can cause so many physical symptoms… and much more.

Making Peace with the End of Life
A clear and comforting guide to help you live well to the last

'Beautifully written – very gentle, personal and not at all frightening – a great resource for both patients and professionals when reassurance is needed.' **Doreen O'Hara, COPD Specialist Nurse**

'A very helpful gathering of advice, support and information for the huge majority who don't know how to navigate the system.' **Dr Rachel Sheils, Consultant in Palliative Medicine**

From GP and hospice doctor Patrick Fitzgerald and bestselling author Sarah Rayner comes a warm and wise companion to help support you and those caring for you in the last months, weeks and days of life.

From the shock of diagnosis, through treatment options and symptom control to the process of dying itself, *Making Peace with the End of Life* tackles these sensitive issues with compassion and honesty. Full of practical advice and important contact information, it will also help to demystify how the NHS and Social Services work, so you can access the best support more easily. And, drawing on Patrick's extensive clinical experience, it also looks at how communicating your wishes to those involved in your care can give a feeling of safety and control over whatever happens in the future.

There are tips on self-nurturing using diet, light exercise and alternative therapies, plus guidance on how to care for your own mental health – including advice for carers.

Offset by Sarah's joyful illustrations, the result is a clear and compassionate guide that aims to make these complex and distressing issues less confusing and overwhelming, so each individual can live the life they have left with a greater sense of comfort and peace.

One Moment, One Morning: A novel

'Carried along by the momentum of a suspense-filled yet touching story that drives to the core of human emotion, this book is a real page-turner, exploring the harrowing pain of loss and grief, family secrets and how a tragic event can force you to be honest about who you really are. A real page-turner ... You'll want to inhale it in one breath.'
Easy Living

The Brighton to London line. The 07:44 train. Carriages packed with commuters. A woman applies her make-up. Another occupies her time observing the people around her. A husband and wife share an affectionate gesture. Further along, a woman flicks through a glossy magazine. Then, abruptly, everything changes: a man has a heart attack, and can't be resuscitated; the train is stopped, an ambulance called. For three passengers on the 07:44 that particular morning, life will never be the same again.

'Touching, insightful, this is a story that will stay with you.'
Take a Break Fiction Feast

'An intimate, thoughtful novel celebrating women's friendship and loyalty.'
Waterstone's Books Quarterly

The Two Week Wait: A novel

What if the thing you most longed for was resting on a two week wait?

After a health scare, Brighton-based Lou learns that her time to have a baby is running out. She can't imagine a future without children, but her partner, Sofia, doesn't seem to feel the same way.

Meanwhile, up in Yorkshire, Cath is longing to start a family with her husband, Rich. No one would be happier to have a child than Rich, but Cath is infertile.

Could these two women help each other out?

'A topical subject treated with insightfulness and care; a wholly absorbing story will prompt a tear or two.' **Easy Living**

'In evoking ordinary lives invaded by a deep, primitive yearning, Rayner's portrayal of her characters interior landscapes is carefully crafted and empathetic.' **The Sunday Times**

'Incredibly compelling... Beautifully written and heartbreakingly honest.' **Novelicious**

Another Night, Another Day: A novel

Three people, each crying out for help . . .

There's Karen, worried about her dying father; Abby, whose son has autism and needs constant care; and Michael, a family man on the verge of bankruptcy. As each sinks under the strain, they're brought together at Moreland's Clinic. Here, behind closed doors, they reveal their deepest secrets, confront and console one another and share plenty of laughs. But how will they cope when a new crisis strikes?

'Written from the heart' **The Bookseller**

'I was engaged and moved by this irresistible novel about friendship, family and dealing with life's blows.' **Woman & Home**

'Brilliant ... Warm and approachable, with fascinating characters.'
Essentials

'Powerful ... A sympathetic insight into the causes and effects of mental ill-health as they affect ordinary people.' **My Weekly**

Printed in Great Britain
by Amazon